Itty Bitty
Amigurumi

50 Quick, Cute, and
Completely No-Sew Crochet Patterns

Itty Bitty Amigurumi

Zac Doar

creator of Crochet me Zaddy

PAGE STREET
PUBLISHING CO.

PAGE STREET
PUBLISHING CO.

First published in 2026 by
Page Street Publishing Co.
27 Congress Street, Suite 1511
Salem, MA 01970
www.pagestreetpublishing.com

Distributed by Macmillan, sales in Canada by The Canadian Manda Group.

30 29 28 27 26   1 2 3 4 5

ISBN-13: 979-8-89003-452-6

Library of Congress Control Number: 2025949644

Edited by Lane Porter
Cover and book design by Emma Hardy for Page Street Publishing Co.
Photography by Anya McInroy and Zac Doar
About the Author photo by Martino Morales

Printed and bound in China

Dedication

To Mum and Dad for always reminding me
to "do what makes you happiest."

Contents

122
124
126
128
130
134
136
138
140
142
146
148
150
152
154
158
160
162
164
166
170
172
174
176
178

Welcome to
Itty Bitty Amigurumi!

This book is an exploration of the small but mighty world of crochet, where the tiniest of stitches come together to create the cutest of critters and friends. Whether you're a seasoned crocheter or just picking up a hook for the first time, this collection of patterns is designed to spark joy and bring a sense of delight to your craft.

My name is Zac, the creator behind Crochet me Zaddy, and I'll be your guide. I've been on the crochet scene for quite some time now. I learned to crochet in 2018 while procrastinating at my old corporate job. One of my team advisors showed me the basics of how to crochet a granny square—shout out to Carole—and I was hooked (pun intended)! I started posting my creations online in the midst of a global pandemic, and the craft community welcomed me with open arms. It was because of their overwhelming support that I have been able to grow as an online force in the crochet world with one of the friendliest, most creative, and most fun-loving communities around me. I've released a multitude of crochet patterns, launched a YouTube channel dedicated to crochet vlogs and tutorials, and created an annual yarn-focused awards event that celebrates online creators and artists in the crafts space. Now, I'm very excitedly publishing my first-ever crochet book.

In this book, you'll find 50 Itty Bitty crochet patterns inspired by wonders big and small from every corner of the universe. From the bustling streets of the city to the tranquil beauty of the garden, each chapter invites you to explore a new theme and bring it to life with your crochet hook.

These patterns are called Itty Bitties because each project has been carefully designed to be quick, cute, and completely no-sew. Each Itty Bitty is the right size to sit comfortably in the cup of your hand, making them perfect for gifting, creating stock for craft fairs, or simply enjoying as a creative outlet. I also opted to use a plush chenille yarn for these designs. Although it's easier to make smaller projects with smaller yarns, the plush chenille yarn gives each design a cute edge and makes sure each Itty Bitty has a soft, squishy, and uniquely playful nature. As an artist, this also created more of a challenge for me, as achieving a small size with a larger yarn is not an easy feat. With fewer stitches to work with, I needed to be precise and considerate about how each design was formed, which I believe is what really sets the Itty Bitty patterns apart from many amigurumi designs done before. The variety of themes ensures there's something here for everyone, whether you love classic farmyard friends, exotic desert dwellers, or even something from the vast expanse of space.

This book is a reminder that even the tiniest creations can bring the biggest smiles and a world of wonder. So, grab your favorite yarn and hook, and let's embark on a journey through the Itty Bitty world of crochet.

Before You Begin

There are no right or wrong ways of doing things in crochet. So much in this craft comes about through trial and error, and fortunately for you, I've already done a lot of the heavy lifting with these patterns . . . Now all that's left is for you to make yourself a cup of tea and settle in for some cozy crochet time.

I always find it helpful when crocheters share the wisdom they have gained along their crafting journeys, and so I thought, "Why don't I do the same?" This chapter shares my top tips and the best advice that I've received over the years, from the essentials of how to read a pattern and the materials you might need before you begin to details like how to properly stuff your plushies to avoid the dreaded lopsided shape! Over time, you will begin to collate your own library of tips and techniques, and I hope this chapter gives you a good starting place.

P.S. If you're more of a visual learner like me and need some video assistance, I've added QR codes throughout so you can access an online library of tutorials.

Reading a Pattern

At first glance, a pattern can look like a complicated mess of letters and numbers—but don't worry; I'm happy to help you out. Each pattern starts off with a list of materials and notions to gather before beginning. Each pattern will contain a list of abbreviations that are used specifically in that project. You can find a full list of these abbreviations on page 23, and the tutorials for each technique begin on page 25.

Then comes the main event: the instructions. Each Itty Bitty has its own step-by-step guide. Each instruction is to be followed from left to right. If there are multiple stitch types in a round, complete all stitches as dictated by the multiplier before each comma before moving on. If there are parentheses around a sequence of stitches, complete this sequence as many times as dictated by the multiplier following the bracketed sequence. The number in parentheses at the end of each round is the total amount of stitches that you should have after that completed round.

Continuous Rounds Versus Working on a Chain

The patterns in this book have been designed to be worked continuously from one round to the next, unless specified as working along a row. When working in the round, do not chain or slip stitch at the beginning or end of a round. When working along a chain, you will need to turn your work and begin working back down the chain starting in a loop as dictated by the pattern. In some cases, you will stitch back into the body and continue working in the round. In other cases, you may turn again and work up the other side of the chain, then proceed to keep working in a continuous round.

Right Side Versus Wrong Side

In crochet, there tends to be two sides to a piece: the right side and the wrong side. Either side can be preferred in different contexts. However, for this book, we will keep the wrong side on the inside of each make! This means that the tail end of your starting knot will always remain on the inside.

Tension

As humans we are all different and unique, and so is our tension when crocheting. Tension refers to the tightness or looseness of your stitches when working with yarn and hook. If your tension is too loose, your plushie may come out floppy, and stuffing could peek through the gaps. If your tension is too tight, your plushie will feel stiff and can be harder to crochet. For amigurumi, a slightly tighter tension than usual works best as it helps create a fabric that is neat and firm—keeping your stitches close together and your critter looking its cutest.

One thing to note when working with the Itty Bitty patterns is that depending on your tension, the placement of certain sculptural stitches may need to be shifted by one or two stitches. For example, in many patterns, bobble stitches are used to represent the legs of the Itty Bitty. If you have a vastly different tension than I do, you may need to alter the placement of your bobble stitches to be one stitch further in the round in order to align them correctly.

That said, after a round that includes bobble stitches, there will sometimes be a round which includes decreases. These decreases may already be assisting in the alignment of the bobble stitches. So, I would suggest seeing how a piece is shaping up first before jumping ahead to align anything differently.

Don't be afraid to experiment and see what placements work best for your tension!

Yarn Over Versus Yarn Under

In crochet, there are two main ways of completing each stitch: a yarn over (YO) or a yarn under (YU). I tend to use YO for a lot of my creations because I naturally have a tight tension. However, some makers prefer to use the YU method as it creates a tighter and more uniform look to their creations. Both techniques are perfectly fine, and it's up to the maker to decide what they are more comfortable with.

Yarn and Tools

In *Itty Bitty Amigurumi*, we use the same notions for every Itty Bitty pattern. If you have the following list of notions with you, you will be able to make every Itty Bitty found in the book.

- Super bulky chenille yarn (variety of colors)
- DK weight black cotton yarn
- 5 mm crochet hook
- Stitch markers
- 12 mm safety eyes
- Darning needle
- Scissors
- Fiber fill stuffing

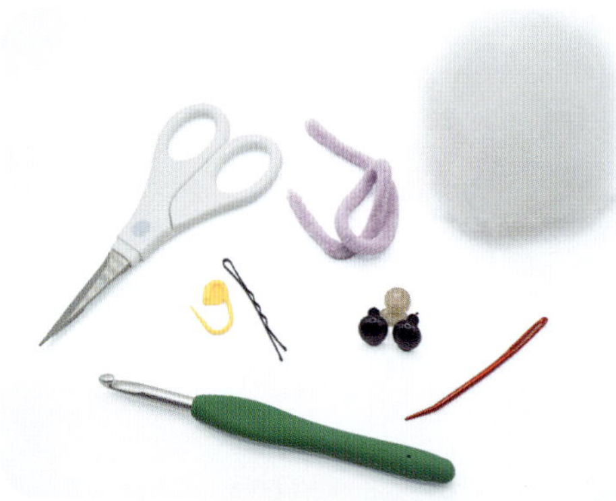

Yarns

All patterns in this book have been created with my own line of yarn, specially crafted for amigurumi projects: A Really Good Chenille Yarn from Zaddycrafts.

This chenille yarn is:

- **Soft and plush**: It's perfect for creating cuddly, huggable critters and designs.

- **Durable**: It's sturdy enough to hold up to everyday handling while retaining its charm.

- **Easy to work with**: Its smooth texture glides effortlessly on your hook, making it ideal for both beginners and seasoned crocheters.

- **Perfect size, weight, and yardage**: At size 6 (Super Bulky), 100 g and 110 m, it's just right for smaller projects.

Using this yarn ensures consistent results and a polished finish for your amigurumi. Plus, the color range is vibrant and varied, so you can always find the perfect shade to suit your project.

Some designs have smaller details. In these instances, I use a DK weight cotton. Usually this will be the Friends Cotton 8/8 from Hobbii. Otherwise, a thin black scrap yarn will work just fine!

While all the patterns in *Itty Bitty Amigurumi* are designed with the size 6 A Really Good Chenille Yarn from Zaddycrafts, they can also be adapted to other yarn types and weights for a variety of effects. If you want to create plushies with different materials, then be aware that you might need to adjust accordingly. For example, if you want to use a chunkier yarn, you will just need a bigger crochet hook and bigger safety eyes to compensate for the size difference!

Using Alternate Yarn Weights

I love using A Really Good Chenille Yarn by Zaddycrafts because it meets all the requirements to make a perfectly soft and squishable plushie. However, the Itty Bitties can work up well using any yarn weight. By adjusting your hook and safety eyes, you can substitute whatever yarn you like. Pictured are some examples of how the scale will change depending on the yarn weight you choose.

From left to right:

1. Yarn weight: Medium weight / Category 4 / Worsted

Suggested hook size: 3 mm

Suggested safety eye size: 8 mm or embroidered

2. Yarn weight: Bulky weight / Category 5 / Chunky

Suggested hook size: 4 mm

Suggested safety eye size: 10 mm or embroidered

3. Yarn weight: Super Bulky / Category 6 / Super Bulky

Suggested hook size: 5 mm

Suggested safety eye size: 12 mm

4. Yarn weight: Jumbo weight / Category 7 / Jumbo

Suggested hook size: 8 mm

Suggested safety eye size: 18 mm

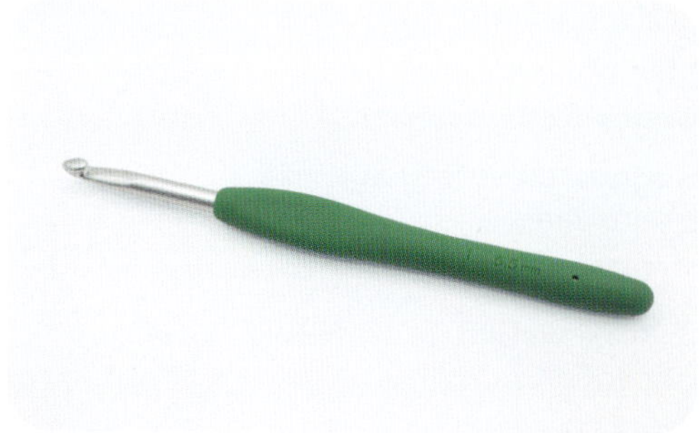

Choosing Your Hook

For all patterns in this book, I suggest starting with a 5 mm hook if you're using A Really Good Chenille Yarn from Zaddycrafts or another size 6 yarn. This size creates tight, defined stitches that are perfect for amigurumi. However, feel free to adjust the hook size slightly to suit your tension or if you are planning to use a different yarn. My favorite hook is from the Clover Amour line. I use a 5 mm hook to account for my tight tension, but many makers will drop to smaller sizes to avoid having any gaps in their stitches—hence 5 mm as a good starting place. As you will be crocheting with the same yarn size for each project, you will only need the one hook for the entirety of this book. Although we use a lighter weight yarn for smaller details on the Itty Bitties, these are made using a darning needle.

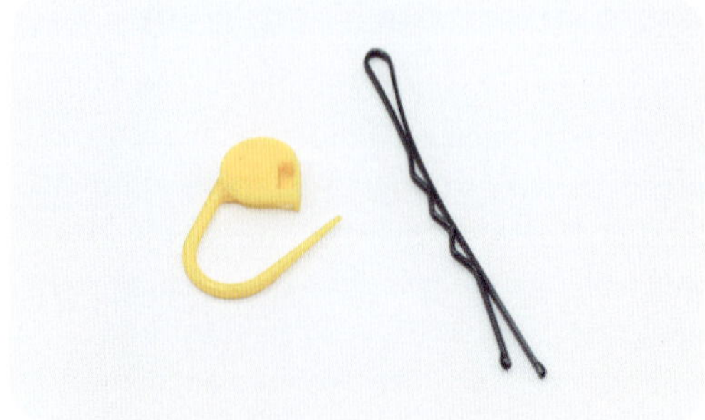

Stitch Markers

I recommend using stitch markers to mark your place as you complete each round. When using chenille yarn, it can be a little tricky to see your stitches—the stitch marker will help you keep track. As a tip, if you make a mistake, you can easily undo your work up until the stitch marker. You will also know you're completing the pattern correctly if you end a round at the stitch marker. I use bobby pins as alternative stitch markers as you can normally get plenty of bobby pins for quite cheap. Some friends use scrap yarn, but it's totally up to you what you're comfortable with.

Safety Eyes

In this book, we like to keep things consistent, and we use just the one size of safety eyes, which is 12 mm. I find this size is the best option for the Itty Bitty designs. You are more than welcome to use other sizes, as different size eyes may look best with your yarn and tension. Please note, however, that if you are intending on gifting or selling your makes to young children, safety eyes can pose a choking hazard and embroidering the eyes might be a better option for you.

Darning Needles

For amigurumi, you will need a darning needle in your notions toolbox. I recommend using a bent-tip metal darning needle as I find this works easily through the bodies of amigurumi pieces as opposed to regular darning needles. The metal also helps avoid any darning needles breaking on you—although some might consider that a rite of passage in the crochet world.

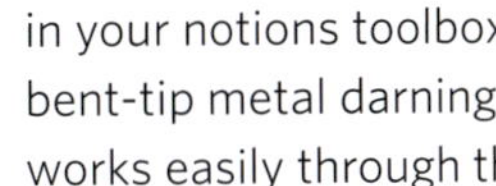

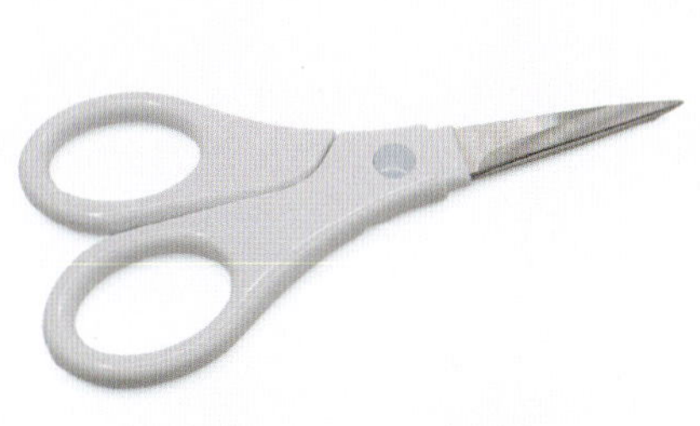

Scissors

Any scissors will do! I prefer smaller scissors as they're easier to carry in a project bag.

Fiber Fill Stuffing

Any fiber fill stuffing brand will do—just whatever you can get your hands on for stuffing the insides of your amigurumi pieces. Personally, I find scrap chenille can be a good filler for some of the pieces, and you'll avoid wasting that yarn.

Sewing and Construction

When working with this book, I wanted to make sure that makers would spend more time crocheting and less time sewing pieces together. Therefore, I have intentionally made every single pattern completely no-sew. There will still be some sewing elements like embroidery, and sewing pieces closed, which are very much unavoidable . . . But sewing pieces together? Zero, zilch, nada, none. (You're welcome!)

Placing Safety Eyes

Each pattern will have directions on where to place safety eyes, which will usually provide the number of stitches between the eyes and in between which rounds the eyes will be placed. I suggest stuffing each plushie a little bit to test how the eyes might look when they're attached to the stuffed plushie. Even if you followed my directions precisely, there are so many factors that can change how the eyes might look on my plushies versus yours—so don't be afraid to take creative liberties and put the eyes where you think they look best!

Stuffing a Plushie

When stuffing a plushie, I always follow the same steps.

1. Fill in any awkward shapes on the plushie, like its arms, legs, snout, etc. and then create a padded layer around the main piece of the plushie.

2. Stuff the center of the plushie and keep stuffing to ensure your plushie will retain its shape. Take care not to overstuff or stretch any stitches.

After closing the piece, it may be necessary to use your hands to squish the plushie into shape. This will allow the stuffing to settle in right.

Scan for a video tutorial!!

Closing Up Your Piece

For most of the projects in this book, there will be a small hole remaining after fastening off from your final round. To close up your piece:

1. Thread the yarn tail left at the end of your project through your darning needle. Insert the needle through each of the front loops of the last round.

2. Pull the yarn tight to close the hole. Weave the yarn tail through the hole and into the body of your project, hiding the remainder of the yarn tail inside.

Abbreviations

st	Stitch
ch	Chain
mc	Magic Circle
sc	Single Crochet
inc	Increase
hdc	Half Double Crochet
hdcinc	Half Double Crochet Increase
dc	Double Crochet
dcinc	Double Crochet Increase
slst	Slip Stitch
FLO/BLO	Front or Back Loops Only
dec	Invisible Decrease
CC	Color Change
B2O/B3O/B4O	Bobble Stitch
CCB2O/CCB3O/CCB4O	Color Changing Bobble Stitch
PS	Picot Stitch
SJoin	Seamless Join Technique
loop	Loop Stitch
ds	Drop Stitch
_in1	Multiple Stitches in One Stitch
HCCsc	Half Color Change Single Crochet
sc3tog	Single Crochet Three Together
TW	Twist Stitch

Techniques

If this is your first time making amigurumi—don't worry, I've got you. I've compiled a small library of tutorials for you showing how to do every stitch you'll need to make each Itty Bitty. I'd suggest getting comfortable with these essential stitches before you start any of the patterns. At the end of this chapter, you will also find some special techniques—feel free to familiarize yourself with these techniques or just refer to the section when necessary.

Essential Techniques

First, let's take a moment to cover the essential crochet techniques you'll see throughout this book. Think of this chapter as your toolkit for the basics of amigurumi.

Stitch

Abbreviation: **st**

When you see "st" in a pattern, it's just short for "stitch." A stitch is one little "V" or loop that you make when you crochet. Every time you pull yarn through to create a new loop, you've made a stitch.

st = one stitch

sts = multiple stitches

So, if your pattern says:

"sc in next available st": Make one single crochet (page 30) into the next available stitch.

"skip 2 sts": You should count two stitches and skip them.

Think of "st" as a quick way for the pattern to say "stitch" without writing the whole word every time!

Slipknot

In this book, a slipknot will only be used if a project begins with a chain stitch.

1. Make a loop with the loose tail crossing underneath the working yarn.

2. Insert your hook into the loop and yarn over with the working yarn.

3. Pull the yarn back through the loop.

4. Holding both tails, pull to tighten the slip knot onto the hook.

Chain ⌄

Abbreviation: **ch**

The chain stitch occurs in only two places in this book: 1) when you are beginning a project, where you will need to make a slipknot prior to chain stitching, or 2) when you are midway through a project, where you will begin chain stitching from the body of the project.

1. Simply take the working yarn and yarn over.

2. Pull the yarn through the existing loop on your hook. This is your first chain stitch.

Repeat as many times as the pattern states.

Scan for a video tutorial!!

Magic Circle >

Abbreviation: **MC**

1. Make a loop and place the loose tail on top of the working yarn.

2. Insert your hook into the loop and grab the working yarn with the hook.

3. Pull the yarn through the loop.

4. Yarn over.

5. Pull the yarn through the loop on your hook.

6. Insert your hook back into the first loop, making sure your hook is also going under the yarn tail.

7. Yarn over and pull through the loop. You should have two loops on your hook.

8. Yarn over and pull through both loops. One loop will remain on your hook. This completes your first single crochet (page 30) in the magic circle.

Repeat steps 4–8 as many times as the pattern states. For example, if your pattern states "MC, 6sc" you will need to complete five more single crochets to reach the 6sc stated in the pattern.

Once you've reached the correct number of stitches in your MC, pull the loose yarn tail to close the circle. You have now completed your magic circle.

Scan for a video tutorial!

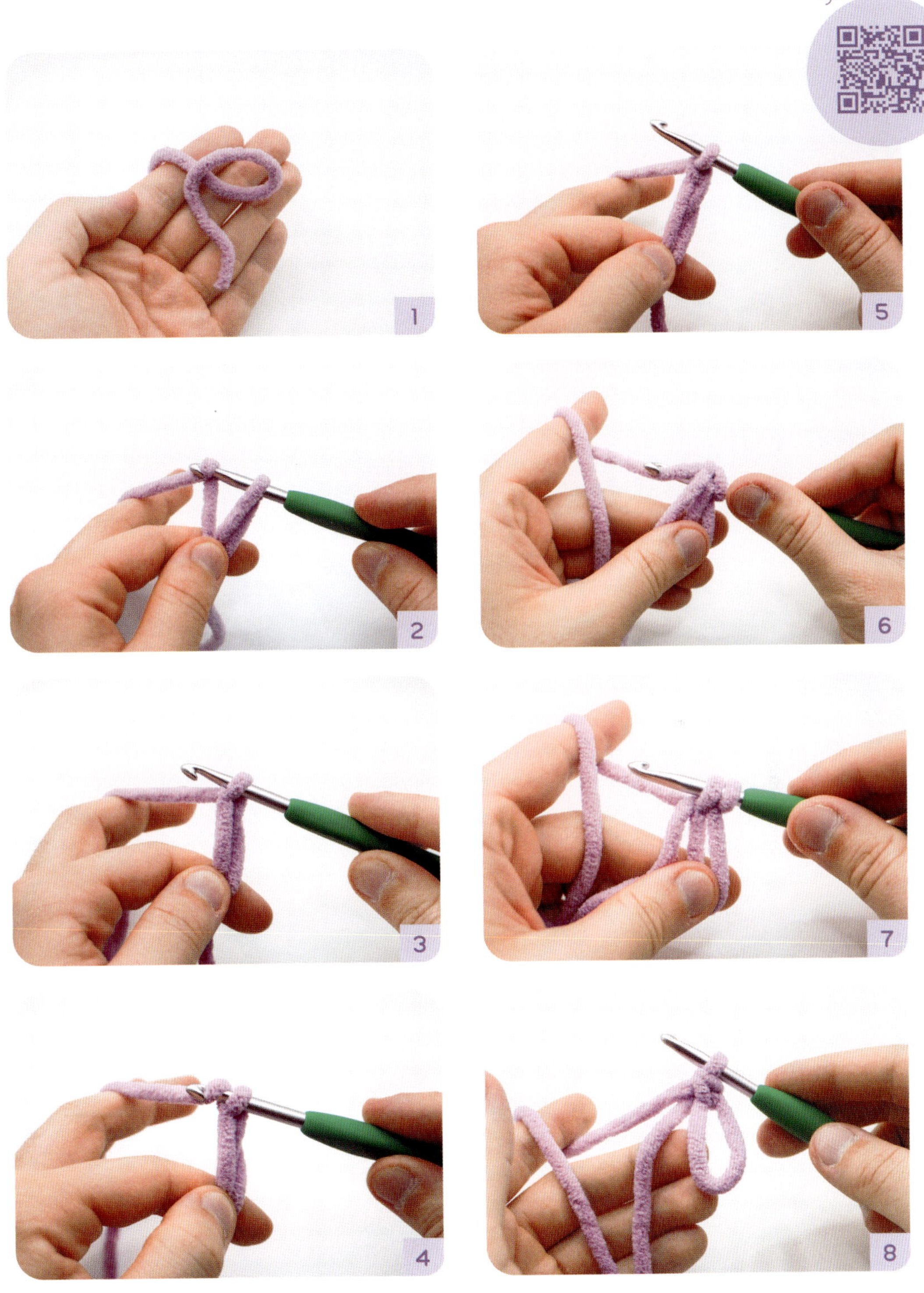

1
2
3
4
5
6
7
8

Single Crochet ‹

Abbreviation: **sc**

1. Insert your hook into a stitch and yarn over.

2. Pull your hook and yarn through the stitch. You should have two loops on your hook. Yarn over.

3. Pull through both loops. One loop will remain on your hook.

Increase ˅

Abbreviation: **inc**

To make an increase, simply complete two single crochets into one stitch. If you refer to the photo, you can see two "V"s in one stitch; that is an increase.

Half Double Crochet ∧

Abbreviation: **hdc**

1. Yarn over.

2. Insert your hook into a stitch.

3. Yarn over and pull your hook and yarn through the stitch. You should have three loops on your hook.

4. Yarn over and pull through all three loops.

Half Double Crochet Increase ∨

Abbreviation: **hdcinc**

To make a half double crochet increase, simply complete two half double crochets in one stitch. If you refer to the photo, you can see two hdcs in one stitch; that is a half double crochet increase.

Double Crochet

Abbreviation: **dc**

1. Yarn over.

2. Insert your hook into a stitch.

3. Yarn over and pull your hook and yarn through the stitch. You should have three loops on your hook.

4. Yarn over and pull through the first two loops only. Two loops will remain on your hook.

5. Yarn over and pull your hook through the remaining two loops. Only one loop will remain on your hook.

Double Crochet Increase ∨

Abbreviation: **dcinc**

To make a double crochet increase, simply complete two double crochets in one stitch. If you refer to the photo, you can see two dcs in one stitch; that is a double crochet increase.

Slip Stitch ∨

Abbreviation: **slst**

1. Insert your hook into a stitch and yarn over.

2. Pull your hook and yarn through the stitch. You should have two loops on your hook.

3. Pull the first loop through the second loop. One loop will remain on your hook.

Front or Back Loops Only ⌄

Abbreviation: **FLO / BLO**

Throughout this book you will find instances where you are asked to work in either the front or the back loops of the next stitches. When you look at your work from above you will see that the stitches look like a series of "V"s. The side closest to you is the front loop and the side furthest away is the back loop. Usually, with each stitch you complete, you will work across both these loops. However, when a pattern states "work in FLO" or "work in BLO" you will work in either loop for as many stitches as stated by the pattern.

For example, when the pattern states "work in BLO: 8sc", you will complete eight single crochets in the next eight back loops only. This means you will be inserting your hook into the center of each "V" and working under the back loop exclusively. After completing these stitches, you will see that there remain eight unused front loops that are visible. Occasionally you will be asked to attach yarn and work into these unused loops, so keep in mind where the unused loops start and consider putting a stitch marker in that loop if necessary.

Invisible Decrease ⌄

Abbreviation: **dec**

A decrease in amigurumi is usually a little different from the standard decrease that is used in flat pieces. As we work in the round, we use an invisible decrease.

1. Insert your hook into the front loops only of the next two stitches. Yarn over and pull through the two front loops. You will have two loops on your hook.

2. Yarn over again and pull through the two remaining loops.

> **Note**: *Occasionally you will be asked to work in the back loops only (BLO) and then decrease (dec). In this circumstance, complete the invisible decrease in the back loops instead of the front loops.*

Working Down the Chain ⌄

Once you have made a series of chain stitches, a pattern may state for you to work down the chain. This means you will work into the loops on one half of your chain. If you were to hold your chain horizontally you will see a row of "V"s. Work into the top loop of each of these "V"s beginning at the second "V" (or chain) from your hook (unless stated otherwise). This is considered working down the chain.

Color Change ⌄

Abbreviation: **CC**

Most of the patterns in this book will require a color change. There are plenty of ways to do this, but because we prefer keeping things simple, we opt for the standard color change.

1. On the last stitch before a color change, insert your hook into the stitch. Yarn over and pull up a loop of your current color. You will have two loops of your original color on your hook. Yarn over in a new color.

2. Pull the new color through both loops on your hook to complete the color change. You will have one loop of the new color remaining on your hook.

There is also a technique for a Color Changing Bobble Stitch, which I will explain further in the special technique section (page 37).

Fasten Off

Once you've finished making a piece of amigurumi, you will need to fasten off your piece. It may sound a little obscure, but in reality, it's very easy.

1. Slip stitch into the next available stitch in the round. (If there's no available stitch, just chain 1.)

2. Lengthen the loop on your hook and cut it.

3. Pull out the working yarn, and lightly pull on the remaining yarn to fasten it.

This leftover length of yarn is your yarn tail.

Special Techniques

In this book, you'll come across many patterns that require a specific crochet stitch or technique as part of the overall design. As these techniques don't occur in every pattern like our essential techniques, we've put them in their own special section.

Bobble Stitch

Abbreviation: **B2O/B3O/B4O**

In this book, the bobble stitch is one of the most reoccurring stitches. The size of the bobble stitch depends on the number of double crochets (page 32) you complete as part of the bobble stitch. To distinguish the size differences, I put the number of dcs in the middle of the classic "BO" abbreviation.

Here is how you complete the three bobble variations that are used in this book:

2 Double Crochet Bobble Stitch (B2O)

1. Yarn over.

2. Insert your hook into the stitch. Yarn over and pull your hook back through the same stitch. There will be three loops on your hook.

3. Yarn over and pull your hook through the first two loops. There will be two loops remaining on your hook.

4. Repeat steps 1–3 once more. There will be three loops remaining on your hook.

5. Yarn over and pull through all loops on your hook. One loop will remain on your hook.

6. Complete the next instructed stitch in the pattern, and this will form the shape of your bobble stitch.

3 Double Crochet Bobble Stitch (B3O)

For this bobble stitch, you will begin with the same first three steps as the 2 Double Crochet Bobble Stitch (page 38) and continue to Step 4 below.

4. Repeat steps 1–3 twice more. There will be four loops remaining on your hook.

5. Yarn over and pull through all loops on your hook. One loop will remain on your hook.

6. Complete the next instructed stitch in the pattern, and this will form the shape of your bobble stitch.

4 Double Crochet Bobble Stitch (B4O)

For this bobble stitch, you will begin with the same first three steps as the 2 Double Crochet Bobble Stitch (page 38) and continue to Step 4 below.

4. Repeat steps 1–3 three times more. There will be five loops remaining on your hook.

5. Yarn over and pull through all loops on your hook. One loop will remain on your hook.

6. Complete the next instructed stitch in the pattern and this will form the shape of your bobble stitch.

Color Changing Bobble Stitch

Abbreviation: **CCB2O/CCB3O/CCB4O**

If a pattern is asking you to color change for a single bobble stitch (page 37), you will do only the bobble stitch portion in the new color and then return to the original color before moving on. This technique is used to avoid any color bleeding around the bobble stitch.

Before starting the bobble stitch, you will still have color one (C1) as the loop on your hook.

1. Yarn over with color 2 (C2).

2. Insert your hook into the stitch. Yarn over with C2 and pull your hook back through the same stitch. There will be three loops remaining on your hook: two in C2 and one in C1.

3. Yarn over with C2 and pull your hook through the first two loops (which are also in C2). There will be two loops remaining on your hook: one in C2 and one in C1.

4. Repeat steps 1–3 a few times more as per your desired bobble stitch size. There will be several loops in C2 and one loop in C1.

5. For the final step, you will yarn over in C1, not C2.

6. Pull through all loops on your hook. You will have one loop remaining in C1 to continue with the pattern.

7. Complete the next instructed stitch in the pattern and this will form the shape of your bobble stitch.

You will see this written in a pattern as "CCB2O: orange." This means you will complete one 2 Double Crochet bobble stitch in orange (C2) and then return to the original color you were using prior to the bobble stitch (C1).

Photos continued on next page

Picot Stitch

Abbreviation: **PS**

In the crochet world, there are many different ways to make a picot stitch. In this book, we only use one variation to make it easier for everyone.

1. Beginning directly from your last completed stitch, make three chain stitches.

2. Complete a single crochet into the third chain loop from your hook.

3. Complete a single crochet into the next available stitch in the round.

Seamless Join Technique >

Abbreviation: **SJoin**

When you have two pieces to join and you want to avoid creating a gap in your work, you can use a seamless join technique. For these instructions, I will refer to the two pieces as piece 1 (P1) and piece 2 (P2). You will have already made P1, and you will be working on P2 when the pattern states that you will SJoin to P1.

When you are joining P2 to P1, you will need to locate two stitches: ST1, the next stitch of your current row on P2, and ST2, the first stitch from the last row of P1.

1. Place both ST1 and ST2 stitches so they face each other.

2. Insert your hook from back to front of ST1, and from the front to back of ST2.

3. Yarn over.

4. Pull through both stitches. You will have two loops remaining on your hook.

5. Yarn over and pull through both loops. You will have one loop remaining on your hook. (If this was supposed to be the last stitch of a round for P2, move your stitch marker to this stitch as it is now the new end of the round.)

6. Insert your hook into ST2 from front to back.

7. Yarn over and pull your hook through the stitch. You will have two loops on your hook.

8. Yarn over and pull through both loops. You will have one loop remaining on your hook.

Scan for a video tutorial!

1
2
3
4
5
6
7
8

Loop Stitch

Abbreviation: **loop**

1. Bring your yarn forward to the front of your project and make a loop that extends about 2 inches (5 cm) in length and returns to the back side of your project. The top end of this loop will be at the base of the previous stitch.

2. Holding the loop in place, crochet over the loop by completing a single crochet into the next available stitch.

3. As pictured, this should lock the loop in place.

Drop Stitch ⌄

Abbreviation: **ds**

1. Insert your hook into the stitch below the next stitch available in the round.

2. Yarn over and pull through your hook. You will have two loops remaining on your hook.

3. Yarn over and pull through both loops. You will have one loop remaining on your hook.

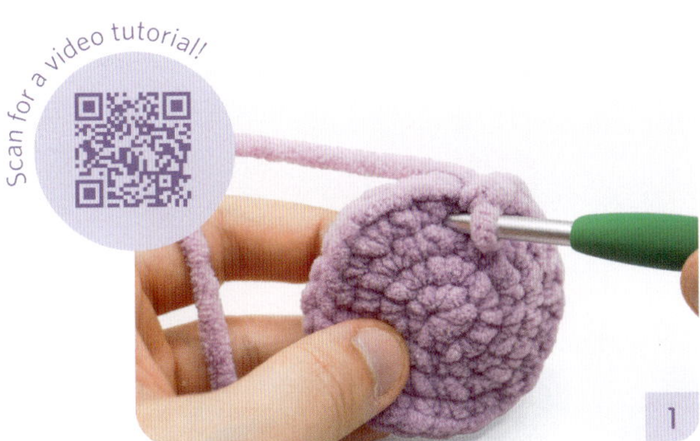

Multiple Stitches in One Stitch ⌄

Abbreviation: **_in1**

In some cases, you will need to complete a variety of stitches in one stitch. This is very similar to a standard increase, but instead you are completing whatever the pattern states in the next stitch. For example: (hdc, dc, hdc)in1 directs you to complete a half double crochet in the stitch, then complete a double crochet in the same stitch, then complete another half double crochet in the same stitch.

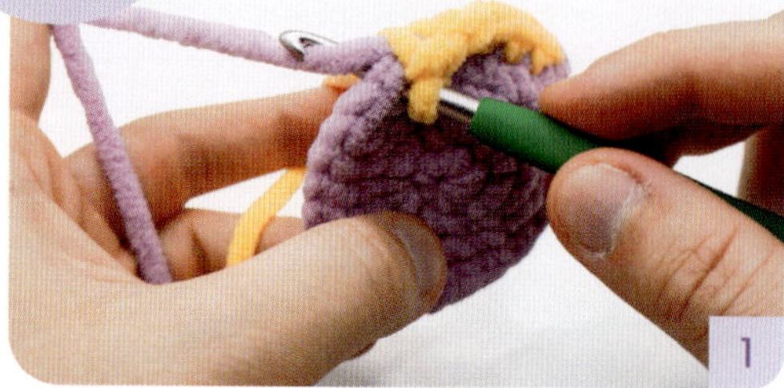

Half Color Change Single Crochet

Abbreviation: **HCCsc**

A half color change single crochet is when the main body of a stitch is in C1, but the color on top is in C2.

1. Insert your hook into the stitch and yarn over with C1.

2. Pull your hook through the stitch. You will have two loops remaining on your hook.

3. Yarn over with C2 and pull through both loops.

4. You will have one loop remaining on your hook in C2.

Single Crochet Three Together

Abbreviation: **sc3tog**

1. Insert your hook into the front loops of the next three stitches. You will have four loops on your hook.

2. Yarn over and pull through the first three loops. You will have two loops on your hook.

3. Yarn over and pull through both loops. You will have one loop left on your hook.

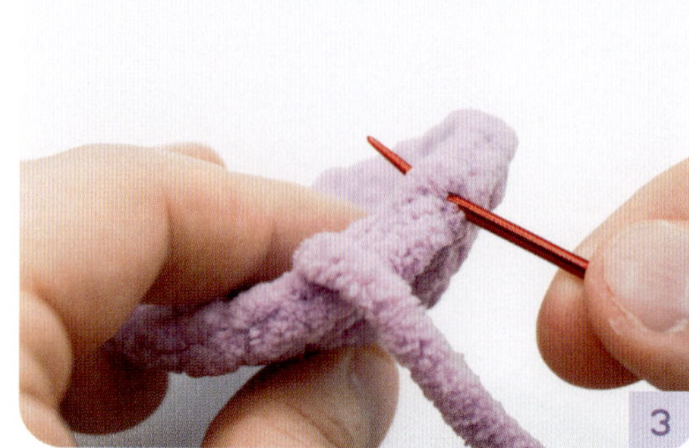

Invisible Fasten Off

1. Complete a regular fasten off (page 36) and insert a yarn tail through your darning needle.

2. Skip one stitch, then pass your needle under both loops of the next stitch.

3. Insert the needle into the center of the last stitch where the yarn tail came out and pass the needle under the back loop.

4. Pull gently to create a "V" shape that mimics the skipped stitch.

Weave the tail into the "wrong side" or simply tuck inside your project when working if possible.

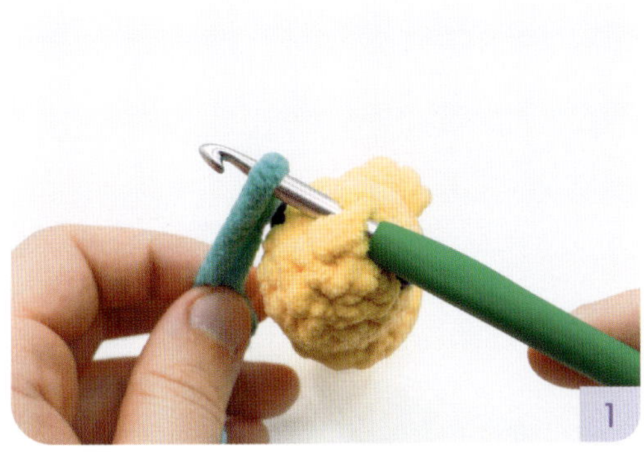

Surface Crochet

Surface crochet on a plushie is a technique where you crochet directly onto the surface of an already completed amigurumi piece.

1. Insert your hook into a stitch or gap on the plushie's surface.

2. Yarn over and pull a loop of yarn through the stitch or gap.

3. Secure with a slip stitch (page 33).

4. Continue working along the surface area using the stitches or gaps as though they were stitches of an unfinished project.

Twist Stitch

Abbreviation: **TW**

1. Extend the loop on your hook until it's about three times the desired length of the twist.

2. Twirl your yarn about 30 times around your hook.

3. Insert your hook into the base of the previous stitch and yarn over. Pull your hook through the stitch and the loop on your hook. You will have one loop remaining on your hook.

4. Complete a single crochet (page 30) into the next available stitch in the round. This will secure the twist.

Crocheting Across Multiple Stitches

As this is a book of completely no-sew patterns, you might be asked to join pieces together or close up a piece using a crochet stitch. In these instances, you will be expected to crochet across stitches.

1. Align the stitches of both pieces that you are crocheting across. Each alignment will make a pair of stitches. If you are joining a piece to the body of a project, make sure the added piece is on the outside of the project.

2. Continue to complete your next crochet stitch as stated by the pattern; however, with each stitch, make sure you insert your hook through both aligned stitches each time.

Repeat this as many times as stated in the pattern.

Finishing Touches

Although *Itty Bitty Amigurumi* is a completely no-sew book when it comes to construction, a small amount of embroidery and fastening really takes these Itty Bitty projects to the next level. Let me show you the most common instances of embroidery in this book so you can feel comfortable with giving it a go yourself.

Creating a Y-Shaped Nose

In some projects you will be expected to embroider a Y-shaped nose.

1. Attach a long piece of yarn to your darning needle.

2. Insert the needle into the plushie, then have it exit between two stitches where you want one top end of the "Y" to start.

3. Have your needle re-enter the plushie in the gap where you want the other top end of the "Y" to be.

4. Repeat steps 2–3 once more.

5. Have the needle exit approximately two stitches below the initial two lines of embroidery.

6. Guide your needle up and underneath the two lines.

7. Making sure you loop over the two lines, have your needle re-enter the plushie in the gap where it last exited.

8. Have the needle exit where you first entered the plushie in step 2. Tug the yarn slightly so it pulls the embroidered lines into a "Y" shape. Tie the starting end to the finishing end. Cut the yarn and tuck the knot inside the plushie.

Scan for a video tutorial!

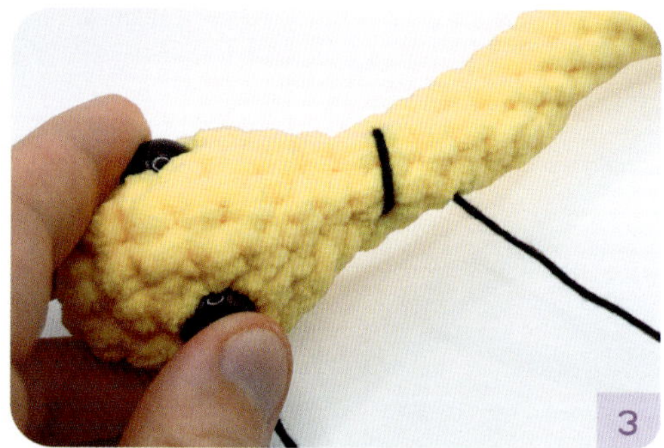

Making a Line

In some projects you will be expected to embroider a straight line. You can use this technique to make stripes, blush, eyebrows, spots, etc.

1. Attach a long piece of yarn to your darning needle. Insert the needle into the plushie, then have it exit between the two stitches where you want the line to start.

2. Have your needle re-enter the plushie in the gap where you want the line to finish.

3. Have the needle exit where you first entered the plushie and tie the starting end to the finishing end. Cut the yarn and tuck the knot inside the plushie.

If you want to make a series of lines, like stripes, use an extra-long piece of yarn and repeat steps 2–3 until you have your desired number of lines. Then fasten off using step 4.

In many cases you will simply need to make two lines on top of each other to create the desired effect of a beak or snout.

Fastening a Piece

In some pieces you will be required to fasten one part of the body to another. It's not necessarily sewing like in traditional amigurumi pieces. It's more just to hold the shape of the piece.

1. Insert a long tail of yarn of the body color you're using into a darning needle and insert the needle inside the body of your Itty Bitty, making sure you exit out at the point where you would like the fastening to happen.

2. Have the needle loop around a stitch of the piece to be fastened, and loop back into the body. Pull the yarn tight to secure both stitches, and therefore pieces, together. Repeat this as many times as needed to keep the pieces secure.

3. Have the needle exit where you first entered the plushie in step 1. Tie the starting end to the finishing end.

4. Cut the yarn and tuck the knot inside the plushie.

Farmyard Friends

Step inside the Itty Bitty farmyard, where the world feels smaller, softer, and infinitely more playful. The barn doors creak open, sunlight spills across straw, and a tiny chorus of clucks and bleats welcomes the day.

Aidan the Cow (page 64) calmly keeps an eye on the day's happenings. Anthony the Goat (page 68) is already halfway up the fence, bleating down to Perry the Pig (page 70), who's splashing happily in a muddy puddle below. Kathryn the Sheep (page 66) sits off to the side, chewing thoughtfully, while Charlie the Chicken (page 62) struts proudly past, looking for a perfect spot to scratch. Together, they make the farm a lively little world of friendship, food, and playful chaos.

Charlie the Chicken

Charlie the Chicken may be small, but this pocket-sized adventurer has a big personality. Always darting around with their best friend, Perry the Pig (page 70), Charlie loves a good adventure, especially if it involves following Perry the Pig's muddy trail. Whether they're exploring the hayloft or pecking around for snacks, these two are inseparable.

Charlie the Chicken is our first critter for a good reason. Here, you'll meet several of the special techniques that pop up throughout the rest of the book, making Charlie a great starter project.

Yarn

- Super bulky weight chenille yarn in three colors: warm white, orange, and red
- Shown in A Really Good Chenille Yarn by ZaddyCrafts in the colorways Simple (warm white), Charisma (orange), and Vibrant (red)

Hook

- 5 mm crochet hook
- Find a full list of notions on page 16, and details for yarn substitutions and hook sizes on page 17.

Special Techniques

- 2dc Bobble Stitch (B2O) (page 38)
- Color Changing Bobble Stitch (CCB2O) (page 41)
- Picot Stitch (PS) (page 43)
- Surface Crochet (page 51)

Charlie the Chicken Pattern

Body

Starting with warm white:

Round 1. MC, 6sc. (6)

Round 2. 6inc. (12)

Round 3. (sc, inc) x 6. (18)

Rounds 4–6. sc around. (3 rounds of 18)

Round 7. 4inc, 2sc, PS, 9sc, PS, sc. (22)

Round 8. sc around. (22)

Round 9. 4dec, 5sc, CCB2O: orange, 2sc, CCB2O: orange, 5sc. (18)

Note: The bobble stitches represent the feet for this Itty Bitty. Due to tension, you may need to adjust their placement so they align properly.

Add the safety eyes between Rounds 4 and 5, with approximately 4 stitches between the eyes.

Start stuffing Charlie the Chicken and continue stuffing as you go.

Round 10. (sc, dec) x 6. (12)

Round 11. dec x 6. (6)

Fasten off the yarn and close up the remaining stitches.

Beak

With orange, embroider a small beak between the two eyes. This should span across 2 stitches and only loop around twice.

Comb

With red, we are going to do some surface crochet. Join your yarn between Rounds 1 and 2 in the middle of Charlie the Chicken's head and then make sure you are working in the stitches towards the back of the plushie.

Row 1. ch2, hdc into the same st where you attached your yarn, 2sc, slst.

Fasten off and weave any yarn tails into the body.

You hatched Charlie the Chicken! Now cluck on over to Aidan the Cow for another farmyard friend.

Aidan the Cow

Aidan the Cow is the steady and wise leader of the barnyard. With a gentle but firm presence, this Itty Bitty guardian keeps everyone in check. Whether it's nudging the goat off the fence or guiding the chicken and pig away from their next cheeky adventure, Aidan the Cow brings a sense of both peace and belonging to the farm, making it a true home for all the animals.

As the first of our four-legged friends, Aidan presents an excellent chance to practice classic color changes as well as to test your tension regarding bobble stitch placement. This Itty Bitty design will help you build confidence in these areas while making one of the cutest and quickest designs in the book.

Yarn

- Super bulky weight chenille yarn in four colors: light pink, warm white, light brown, and black
- Shown in A Really Good Chenille Yarn by ZaddyCrafts in the colorways Sweet (light pink), Simple (warm white), Gentle (light brown), and Mischief (black)

Hook

- 5 mm crochet hook
- Find a full list of notions on page 16, and details for yarn substitutions and hook sizes on page 17.

Special Techniques

- 2dc Bobble Stitch (B2O) (page 38)
- 3dc Bobble Stitch (B3O) (page 39)
- Color Changing Bobble Stitch (CCB2O) (page 41)
- Multiple Stitches in One Stitch (_in1) (page 47)
- Picot Stitch (PS) (page 43)

Aidan the Cow Pattern

Starting with light pink:

Round 1. ch4. (4)

Turn and work back down the ch, starting in the second ch from your hook. We will be working in this chain in the round as opposed to individual rows.

Round 2. (2sc, 3scin1) x 2. (10)

Round 3. sc around. (10)

Round 4. CC to warm white: 5sc, 2inc, 3sc. (12)

Round 5. (sc, inc) x 6. (18)

Round 6. (5sc, inc) x 3. (21)

Round 7. B3O, 4sc, B3O, 4sc, ch4, work down the chain starting in the third chain from your hook, hdc, sc, sc into next available st of the body, CCB2O: light brown, 3sc, CCB2O: light brown (However, pull through a loop of black instead of warm white upon completion of the Color Changing Bobble Stitch.) sc, ch4, work down the chain starting in the third chain from your hook, hdc, sc, sc into next available st of the body, sc, CC to warm white: 2sc. (21)

Note: The bobble stitches represent the legs for this Itty Bitty. Due to tension, you may need to adjust their placement so they align properly.

Round 8. 16sc, CC to black: 3sc, CC to warm white: 2sc. (21)

Rounds 9–10. sc around. (2 rounds of 21)

Round 11. 10sc, CC to black: 3sc, CC to warm white: 8sc. (21)

Add the safety eyes between Rounds 5 and 6, with approximately 6 stitches between the eyes.

Start stuffing Aidan the Cow and continue stuffing as you go.

Round 12. sc, B3O, 3sc, B3O, 4sc, CC to black: 3sc, CC to warm white: 8sc. (21)

Round 13. (5sc, dec) x 3. (18)

Round 14. (sc, dec) x 6. (12)

Round 15. 4dec, sc, PS, dec. (7)

Fasten off the yarn and close up the remaining stitches.

Moo-velous! Aidan the cow is done. Shall we meet Kathryn the Sheep next?

Kathryn the Sheep

Kathryn the Sheep is the barnyard's peaceful soul, content to graze in the sunshine or nap under a shady tree. They bring calm in the midst of Anthony the Goat's (page 68) chaos and Perry the Pig's (page 70) excitement. When the barnyard gets too noisy, you can always count on this sheep to bring the vibe back to mellow.

Kathryn the Sheep is the best project for practicing the bobble stitch. This pattern keeps things simple while still giving you that fluffy texture in a small, manageable package.

Yarn

- Super bulky weight chenille yarn in two colors: light gray and warm white
- DK weight cotton yarn in black
- Shown in A Really Good Chenille Yarn by ZaddyCrafts in the colorways Charming (light gray) and Simple (warm white), and Friends Cotton 8/8 by Hobbii in Black

Hook

- 5 mm crochet hook
- Find a full list of notions on page 16, and details for yarn substitutions and hook sizes on page 17.

Special Techniques

- 2dc Bobble Stitch (B2O) (page 38)
- 3dc Bobble Stitch (B3O) (page 39)
- Color Changing Bobble Stitch (CCB3O) (page 41)

Kathryn the Sheep Pattern

Body

Starting with light gray:

Round 1. MC, 6sc. (6)

Round 2. (sc, inc) x 3. (9)

Round 3. 3inc, 6sc. (12)

Round 4. 6inc, 6sc. (18)

Round 5. (5sc, inc) x 3. (21)

Round 6. CC to warm white and work in BLO: slst, CC to light gray and work in both loops: sc, ch3, sc into second ch from hook, work down the ch: slst, sc into next available st on the body, CC to warm white and work in BLO: 8slst, CC to light gray and work in both loops: sc, ch3, sc into second ch from hook, work down the ch: slst, sc into next available st on the body, CC to warm white and work in BLO: 8slst. (21)

Round 7. Work in BLO: sc, work in both loops: 2sc, work in BLO: (sc, B2O) x 4, work in both loops: 2sc, work in BLO: 2sc, CCB3O: light gray, 3sc, CCB3O: light gray, sc. (21)

Note: The bobble stitches represent the legs for this Itty Bitty. Due to tension, you may need to adjust their placement so they align properly.

Round 8. Work in both loops: (sc, B2O) x 7, 7sc. (21)

Round 9. (B2O, sc) x 8, 5sc. (21)

Round 10. (sc, B2O) x 7, 7sc. (21)

Round 11. (B2O, sc) x 8, CCB3O: light gray, 2sc, CCB3O: light gray, sc. (21)

Add the safety eyes between Rounds 4 and 5, with approximately 3 stitches between the eyes.

Start stuffing Kathryn the Sheep and continue stuffing as you go.

Round 12. (B2O, dec) x 6, sc, dec. (14)

Round 13. 7dec. (7)

Fasten off the yarn and close up the remaining stitches.

Nose

Using black cotton yarn, embroider a small nose between the two eyes. This should span across 2 stitches and only loop around twice. Make sure you do a singular loop from the bottom, pulling it softly to create a small "Y" shape.

Baa-mazing work! You've finished Kathryn the Sheep. Anthony the Goat is next, waiting to join the herd.

Anthony the Goat

Anthony the Goat is the farm's cheeky pint-sized troublemaker. Always climbing where they shouldn't, nibbling things they shouldn't, and generally stirring up commotion, Anthony's antics keep the barnyard lively. This Itty Bitty rascal may be mischievous, but their playful spirit makes them impossible not to love.

Anthony's design is straightforward, with minimal color changes, and is one of the only cases where you are almost sewing during a project. A great Itty Bitty choice when you want something quick, low-effort, and maybe want to explore the idea of sewing again.

Anthony the Goat Pattern

Body

Starting with light brown:

Round 1. MC, 6sc. (6)

Round 2. (sc, inc) x 3. (9)

Round 3. 3inc, 6sc. (12)

Round 4. 6inc, 6sc. (18)

Round 5. (5sc, inc) x 3. (21)

Round 6. 3sc, ch5, work back down the ch starting in the third loop from the hook: dc, hdc, sc, sc in next st of the Body, CCB3O: light gray, 4sc, CCB3O: light gray, sc, ch5, work back down the ch starting in the third loop from the hook: dc, hdc, sc, sc in next st of the Body, 3sc, B3O, 3sc, B3O, sc. (21)

Note: The bobble stitches represent the legs for this Itty Bitty. Due to tension, you may need to adjust their placement so they align properly.

Round 7. sc around. (21)

Round 8. 4sc, 3dec, 11sc. (18)

Rounds 9–10. sc around. (2 rounds of 18)

Round 11. 14c, B3O, 2sc, B3O. (18)

Add the safety eyes between Rounds 4 and 5, with approximately 4 stitches between the eyes.

Start stuffing Anthony the Goat and continue stuffing as you go.

Round 12. (sc, dec) x 6. (12)

Round 13. 2dec, sc, PS, 3dec. (6)

Fasten off the yarn and close up the remaining stitches.

Using a long tail of light brown yarn, fasten the edges of the ears to the sides of the body.

Nose

Using black cotton yarn, embroider a small nose between the two eyes. This should span across 2 stitches and only loop around twice. Make sure you do a singular loop from the bottom, pulling it softly to create a small "Y" shape.

Anthony the Goat, or should I say, Anthony the G.O.A.T.? Now crochet Perry the Pig to round out our barnyard crew.

Perry the Pig is the barnyard's fun-loving ball of energy, and they wouldn't dream of going on an adventure without Charlie the Chicken (page 62) by their side. Together, they may be small, but they are the dynamic duo of the farm, always finding new ways to keep things lively. Mud puddles, hay forts, and impromptu races around the barn: They're all part of the duo's playbook.

Perry the Pig introduces one new special technique: the twist stitch (page 52). New techniques aren't something to be avoided, but something to be embraced. The rest of the pattern remains simple and beginner-friendly as it's a quick Itty Bitty make that's as cute as it is approachable.

Perry the Pig Pattern

Body

Starting with hot pink:

Round 1. ch4. (4)

Round 2. Work down the ch starting in the second loop from the hook: 2sc, 3scin1, turn your work and continue working into the other side of your initial ch: 2sc, 3scin1. (10)

Round 3. sc around. (10)

Round 4. CC to light pink: 5sc, 2inc, 3sc. (12)

Round 5. (sc, inc) x 6. (18)

Round 6. (5sc, inc) x 3. (21)

Round 7. B3O, 3sc, B3O, 6sc, PS, 3sc, PS, 5sc. (21)

Note: The bobble stitches represent the legs for this Itty Bitty. Due to tension, you may need to adjust their placement so they align properly.

Rounds 8–11. sc around. (4 rounds of 21)

Round 12. sc, B3O, 2sc, B3O, 16sc. (21)

Add the safety eyes between Rounds 5 and 6, with approximately 4 stitches between the eyes.

Start stuffing Perry the Pig and continue stuffing as you go.

Round 13. (5sc, dec) x 3. (18)

Round 14. (sc, dec) x 6. (12)

Round 15. 4dec, slst, TW, dec. (7)

Fasten off the yarn and close up the remaining stitches.

Nostrils

Using a small amount of black cotton yarn, embroider two small vertical lines on the snout of Perry the Pig.

Oink-credible! You finished Perry the Pig and the whole farmyard chapter! Time to graze your way into the next adventure.

Woodland Wonders

Here in the Itty Bitty woodlands, the forest feels like nature's dollhouse, with pockets of moss, trickles of light, and tiny critters darting between the trees. Each flutter, rustle, and whisper of wind becomes part of a small, magical story unfolding all around you.

Zac the Squirrel (page 78) darts nimbly between branches, hiding acorns in the log that Matthias the Mushroom (page 82) sits upon. Hollie the Hedgehog (page 74) bumbles through a carpet of leaves searching for berries, while Aspen the Owl (page 76) keeps watch from above. Yohei the Fox (page 80) slips through the undergrowth mischievously, looking out for whom they should prank next.

Hollie the Hedgehog

With tiny paws that tread quietly over mossy ground, Hollie the Hedgehog spends their evenings collecting nature's gifts: delicate flowers, bright berries, and shiny pebbles washed in the stream. A gentle, quiet soul, this Itty Bitty hedgehog loves to stop by Matthias the Mushroom (page 82) for the latest woodland news.

This pattern introduces the drop stitch (page 47), a fun new technique that creates Hollie's spiky look. Although it may look complex, it's still a simple, quick, beginner-friendly make, perfect for branching out and learning new techniques in crochet.

Yarn

- Super bulky weight chenille yarn in two colors: light brown and brown
- Shown in A Really Good Chenille Yarn by ZaddyCrafts in the colorways Gentle (light brown) and Cuddly (brown)

Hook

- 5 mm crochet hook
- Find a full list of notions on page 16, and details for yarn substitutions and hook sizes on page 17.

Special Techniques

- 2dc Bobble Stitch (B2O) (page 38)
- Color Changing Bobble Stitch (CCB2O) (page 41)
- Drop Stitch (ds) (page 47)

Hollie the Hedgehog Pattern

Body

Starting with light brown:

Round 1. MC, 6sc. (6)

Round 2. (sc, inc) x 3. (9)

Round 3. 3inc, 6sc. (12)

Round 4. 6inc, 6sc. (18)

Round 5. (5sc, inc) x 3. (21)

Round 6. CC to brown: slst, 20sc. (21)

Round 7. (ds, sc) x 8, CCB2O: light brown, 3sc, CCB2O: light brown. (21)

> **Note:** The bobble stitches represent the legs for this Itty Bitty. Due to tension, you may need to adjust their placement so they align properly.

Round 8. (sc, ds) x 8, 5sc. (21)

Round 9. (ds, sc) x 8, 5sc. (21)

Round 10. (sc, ds) x 8, 5sc. (21)

Round 11. (ds, sc) x 8, ds, CCB2O: light brown, 2sc, CCB2O: light brown. (21)

Add the safety eyes between Rounds 4 and 5, with approximately 5 stitches between the eyes. The B2Os from Rounds 7 and 11 should be in the bottom of the body.

Start stuffing Hollie the Hedgehog and continue stuffing as you go.

Round 12. (sc, ds) x 8, 5sc. (21)

Round 13. (ds, sc) x 2, ds, dec, (sc, ds) x 2, sc, dec, (ds, sc) x 2, sc, dec. (18)

Round 14. (sc, ds) x 3, (ds, sc) x 2, ds, (ds, sc) x 2, 3ds. (18)

Round 15. dec x 9. (9)

Fasten off the yarn and close up the remaining stitches.

Nose

Using brown yarn, embroider a small nose on the front of the Hollie the Hedgehog.

Hollie the Hedgehog is all curled up and complete! Next up, wise old Aspen the Owl!

Aspen the Owl

Aspen the Owl claims to have seen it all and tells stories like they truly have. Their yarns are stitched together with equal parts fact, exaggeration, and complete nonsense, but in reality, no one minds. From the secrets of the squirrel's acorn stash to the fox's latest prank, nothing in the woodlands can escape being turned into an epic tale when this Itty Bitty owl has a captive audience.

Aspen is a great chance to practice color changes. There are a few to keep you on your toes, but nothing too tricky apart from maybe a singular half color change. This makes Aspen the perfect Itty Bitty project to put earlier skills into action, while also getting a taste of more complex techniques.

Yarn

- Super bulky weight chenille yarn in three colors: brown, warm white, and light brown
- Shown in A Really Good Chenille Yarn by ZaddyCrafts in the colorways Cuddly (brown), Simple (warm white), and Gentle (light brown)

Hook

- 5 mm crochet hook
- Find a full list of notions on page 16, and details for yarn substitutions and hook sizes on page 17.

Special Techniques

- 2dc Bobble Stitch (B2O) (page 38)
- Color Changing Bobble Stitch (CCB2O) (page 41)
- Half Color Change Single Crochet (HCCsc) (page 48)
- Picot Stitch (PS) (page 43)

Aspen the Owl Pattern

Body

Starting with brown:

Round 1. MC, 6sc. (6)

Round 2. 6inc. (12)

Round 3. sc, inc, sc, PS, sc in same st, (sc, inc) x 2, sc, PS, sc in same st, sc, inc. (18)

Round 4. sc around. (18)

Round 5. 5sc, CC to warm white, 3sc, HCCsc: pull through a loop of brown followed by pulling a loop of warm white through both loops to complete, 3sc, CC to brown: 6sc. (18)

Round 6. 5sc, CC to warm white: 7sc, CC to brown: 6sc. (18)

Round 7. 4sc, PS, CC to warm white: 7sc, CC to brown: sc, PS, 4sc. (18)

Rounds 8-9. sc around. (2 rounds of 18)

Round 10. 6sc, CCB2O: light brown, 4sc, CCB2O: light brown, 6sc. (18)

> **Note:** The bobble stitches represent the feet for this Itty Bitty. Due to tension, you may need to adjust their placement so they align properly.

Add the safety eyes between Rounds 6 and 7, with approximately 4 stitches between the eyes. The HCCsc will line up with the center of the eyes.

Start stuffing Aspen the Owl and continue stuffing as you go.

Round 11. (sc, dec) x 6. (12)

Round 12. 6dec. (6)

Fasten off and close up the remaining stitches.

Beak

With light brown yarn, embroider a small beak between the two eyes, between Rounds 6 and 7. This should span across 2 stitches and only loop around twice.

Hoot-hoot! Ahem. I mean, whoop whoop! Aspen the Owl is all done! Let's fly on over to make Zac the Squirrel.

Zac the Squirrel

Zac the Squirrel is the woodland's smallest socialite, darting between trees and making friends everywhere they go. Quick, curious, and endlessly chatty, this Itty Bitty squirrel can turn even a simple branch into a stage for dramatic storytelling.

Overall, this is a relatively quick and simple make. Zac does, however, introduce a joining technique for the first time. It's an exciting skill to add to your crochet skill toolkit, and the payoff is well worth it.

Yarn

- Super bulky weight chenille yarn in two colors: brown and light brown
- Shown in A Really Good Chenille Yarn by ZaddyCrafts in the colorways Cuddly (brown) and Gentle (light brown)

Hook

- 5 mm crochet hook
- Find a full list of notions on page 16, and details for yarn substitutions and hook sizes on page 17.

Special Techniques

- 2dc Bobble Stitch (B2O) (page 38)
- Picot Stitch (PS) (page 43)
- Surface Crochet (page 51)

Zac the Squirrel Pattern

Tail

Starting with brown:

Round 1. MC, 6sc. (6)

Rounds 2-5. sc around. (4 rounds of 6)

Round 6. sc, tightly roll the Tail so that Round 5 is now adjacent to Round 2. Directly surface crochet 2sc into the middle of Round 2. sc back into the 4 st from Round 5, 2sc. (6)

You will now continue to crochet in the round using the 2 stitches from the surface crochet in Round 6.

Rounds 7-10. sc around. (4 rounds of 6)

Do not stuff the tail.

Round 11. Flatten the piece and 3sc across. Every sc will go across 2 stitches. (3)

Fasten off and weave in any yarn tails.

Body

Starting with light brown:

Round 1. MC, 6sc. (6)

Round 2. 2inc, PS, sc in same st, inc, PS, sc in same st, inc. (12)

Round 3. (sc, inc, sc) x 4. (16)

Rounds 4-5. sc around. (2 rounds of 16)

Round 6. 7sc, 2inc, 7sc. (18)

Round 7. sc around. (18)

Round 8. 4sc, 6dec, 2sc. (12)

Round 9. Work in FLO: (sc, inc, sc) x 4. (16)

Add the safety eyes between Rounds 4 and 5, with approximately 4 stitches between the eyes.

Start stuffing Zac the Squirrel and continue stuffing as you go.

Round 10. 7sc, B2O, 3sc, B2O, 4sc. (16)

Round 11. sc around. (16)

Round 12. sc, next join the tail by completing 3sc through both the edge of the tail and the next 3 sts of the body, 3sc, B2O, 3sc, B2O, 4sc. (16)

Round 13. 8dec. (8)

Fasten off the yarn and close up the remaining stitches.

Using a long tail of light brown yarn, fasten the tail to the back of the body so it sits upright.

Nose

Using brown yarn, embroider a small nose between the two eyes. This should span across 2 stitches and only loop around twice. Make sure you do a singular loop from the bottom, pulling it softly to create a small "Y" shape.

Job acorn-plished! Zac the Squirrel is finished! Now we need a friend to scurry around with. How about Yohei the Fox?

Yohei the Fox

Yohei the Fox has a twinkle in their eye and more tricks than their tiny paws can carry. They're a night wanderer by nature, slipping through silver-lit meadows with a mischievous grin, but by day, you'll find them stretched out in the meadow sunbathing with their friends. This Itty Bitty fox keeps the woodland lively and full of fun.

Yohei uses several color changes, but the steps are simple and beginner friendly. They're an easy Itty Bitty project that rewards you with a character full of personality.

Yarn

- Super bulky weight chenille yarn in three colors: orange, warm white, and black
- DK weight cotton yarn in black
- Shown in A Really Good Chenille Yarn by ZaddyCrafts in the colorways Charisma (orange), Simple (warm white), and Mischief (black), and Friends Cotton 8/8 by Hobbii in Black

Hook

- 5 mm crochet hook
- Find a full list of notions on page 16, and details for yarn substitutions and hook sizes on page 17.

Special Techniques

- 3dc Bobble Stitch (B3O) (page 39)
- Color Changing Bobble Stitch (CCB3O) (page 41)
- Picot Stitch (PS) (page 43)

Yohei the Fox Pattern

Body

Starting with orange:

Round 1. MC, 3sc, CC to warm white: 3sc. (6)

Round 2. CC to orange: 3sc, CC to warm white: 3inc. (9)

Round 3. CC to orange: 3inc, CC to warm white: 6sc. (12)

Round 4. CC to orange: 6inc, CC to warm white: 6sc. (18)

Round 5. CC to orange: (5sc, inc) x 3. (21)

Round 6. 5sc, PS, 4sc, PS, 4sc, CCB3O: black, 3sc, CCB3O: black, sc. (21)

Note: The bobble stitches represent the legs for this Itty Bitty. Due to tension, you may need to adjust their placement so they align properly.

Round 7. sc around. (21)

Round 8. 5sc, 3dec, 10sc. (18)

Rounds 9–11. sc around. (3 rounds of 18)

Round 12. 14sc, CCB3O: black, 2sc, CCB3O: black. (18)

Add the safety eyes between Rounds 4 and 5, with approximately 4 stitches between the eyes.

Start stuffing Yohei the Fox and continue stuffing as you go.

Round 13. (sc, dec) x 6. (12)

Round 14. 6dec. (6)

Round 15. (sc, inc) x 3. (9)

Rounds 16–17. sc around. (2 rounds of 9)

Round 18. CC to warm white: (sc, dec) x 3. (6)

Round 19. sc around. (6)

Fasten off the yarn and close up the remaining stitches.

Nose

Using black cotton yarn, embroider a small nose on the end of the snout. This should span across 2 stitches and only loop around twice. Make sure you do a singular loop from the bottom, pulling it softly to create a small "Y" shape.

Fantastic fox! Yohei is done, so now let's scamper on over to Matthias the Mushroom.

Matthias the Mushroom

Matthias the Mushroom sits like a tiny guardian on their fallen log, the perfect seat for a pocket-sized observer. From this little throne, they overhear every squirrel's chatter and fox's mischief, with an occasional owl dropping by to add to the tale. Friends come not just for the latest gossip but for the calm, steady comfort of Matthias's welcoming presence.

One of the simplest designs in this chapter, Matthias is perfect for practicing your stitches. They're a quick Itty Bitty make that gives maximum charm with minimal effort.

Matthias the Mushroom Pattern

Mushroom Cap

Starting with red:

Round 1. MC, 6sc. (6)

Round 2. (sc, inc) x 3. (9)

Round 3. (sc, inc, sc) x 3. (12)

Round 4. (sc, inc, sc) x 4. (16)

Round 5. Work in FLO: (sc, inc) x 8. (24)

Rounds 6-7. sc around. (2 rounds of 24) Fasten off with an Invisible Fasten Off into the first st of Round 7 and weave in any yarn tails.

Using warm white yarn, attach to the first unused back loop remaining from Round 5.

Round 8. sc around in each of the back loops from Round 5. (16)

Round 9. (3sc, inc) x 4. (20)

Rounds 10-13. sc around. (4 rounds of 20)

Add the safety eyes between Rounds 11 and 12, with approximately 3 stitches between the eyes.

Start stuffing Matthias the Mushroom and continue stuffing as you go.

Round 14. (3sc, dec) x 4. (16)

Round 15. dec x 8. (8)

Fasten off and close up the remaining stitches.

Spots

Using warm white yarn, embroider a series of small spots on the mushroom cap. If you're finding that your mushroom cap is flipping upwards, use the embroidery spots to anchor the mushroom cap down onto the body.

You sprouted Matthias the Mushroom! And with that the woodland chapter is complete—well done! I wonder where we'll go next?

ZOO
LION
RHINO

Day at the Zoo

Welcome to the Itty Bitty zoo, where every corner hums with tiny bursts of energy and the air buzzes with a cheerful chorus of small but mighty voices. The winding paths here don't lead to grand exhibits, but to pocket-sized habitats where every small friend brings a quirk that stitches the zoo into a lively little world.

Bethany the Giraffe (page 88) stretches up high for the freshest leaves while Millie the Monkey (page 90) darts through the canopies, swinging with glee. Rhiannon the Rhino (page 92) plods alongside Ali the Elephant (page 86), and neither of them can resist a splash in the pool. All the while, Dzmitry the Lion (page 94) basks in the rays of a sunny day, seemingly asleep but always keeping track of the day's adventures.

Ali the Elephant

Ali the Elephant is the heart of the zoo's support network. This Itty Bitty elephant has a gift for making every friend feel seen and cared for, whether it's by lending a steady trunk to help Bethany the Giraffe (page 88) reach that last leafy snack, or quietly walking beside Rhiannon the Rhino (page 92) on slow, peaceful laps of the enclosure. They are a great listener and their kind presence brings the whole group together.

Ali introduces a fun new way to crochet curves. It's a fresh technique but still approachable, making this Itty Bitty elephant both a delight to stitch and a great learning opportunity for those who might want to explore designing their own crochet pieces one day.

Yarn

- Super bulky weight chenille yarn in light blue
- Shown in A Really Good Chenille Yarn by ZaddyCrafts in the colorway Spirited (light blue)

Hook

- 5 mm crochet hook
- Find a full list of notions on page 16, and details for yarn substitutions and hook sizes on page 17.

Special Techniques

- 3dc Bobble Stitch (B3O) (page 39)
- Multiple Stitches in One Stitch (_in1) (page 47)

Ali the Elephant Pattern

Starting with light blue:

Round 1. MC, 5sc. (5)

Round 2. sc around. (5)

Round 3. Work in BLO: 2sc, work in both loops: 3sc.

Round 4. Work in the unused front loops from Round 3: 2sc, work in both loops: 3sc.

Round 5. Work in BLO: 2sc, work in both loops: 3sc.

Round 6. Work in the unused front loops from Round 5: 2sc, work in both loops: 3sc.

Round 7. 5inc. (10)

Round 8. (sc, inc) x 5. (15)

Round 9. (sc, inc, sc) x 5. (20)

Round 10. 13sc, B3O, 3sc, B3O, 2sc. (20)

Note: The bobble stitches represent the legs for this Itty Bitty. Due to tension, you may need to adjust their placement so they align properly.

Round 11. sc, work in FLO: (hdc, dc)in1, (2dc)in1, (dc, hdc)in1, work in both loops: 3sc, work in FLO: (hdc, dc)in1, (2dc)in1, (dc, hdc)in1, work in both loops: 10sc. (20*)

*Do not count the sts from the front loops as we will work into the back loops in the next round.

Round 12. sc, work in the unused back loops from Round 11: 3sc, work in both loops: 3sc, work in the unused back loops from Round 11: 3sc, work in both loops: 10sc. (20)

Rounds 13–14. sc around. (2 rounds of 20)

Round 15. 15sc, B3O, 2sc, B3O, sc. (20)

Add the safety eyes between Rounds 8 and 9, with approximately 3 stitches between the eyes. The trunk of the elephant should naturally point up between these and the ears.

Start stuffing Ali the Elephant and continue stuffing as you go, but don't stuff the trunk.

Round 16. (4sc, dec, 4sc) x 2. (18)

Round 17. (sc, dec) x 6. (12)

Round 18. sc, dec, sc, ch5, work down the chain starting in the second loop from the hook: 4slst, sc into the next available st of the body, dec, sc, 2dec. (8)

Fasten off the yarn and close up the remaining stitches.

Fantastic! Ali the Elephant is finished. Let's go stretch out with our friend Bethany the Giraffe.

Bethany the Giraffe

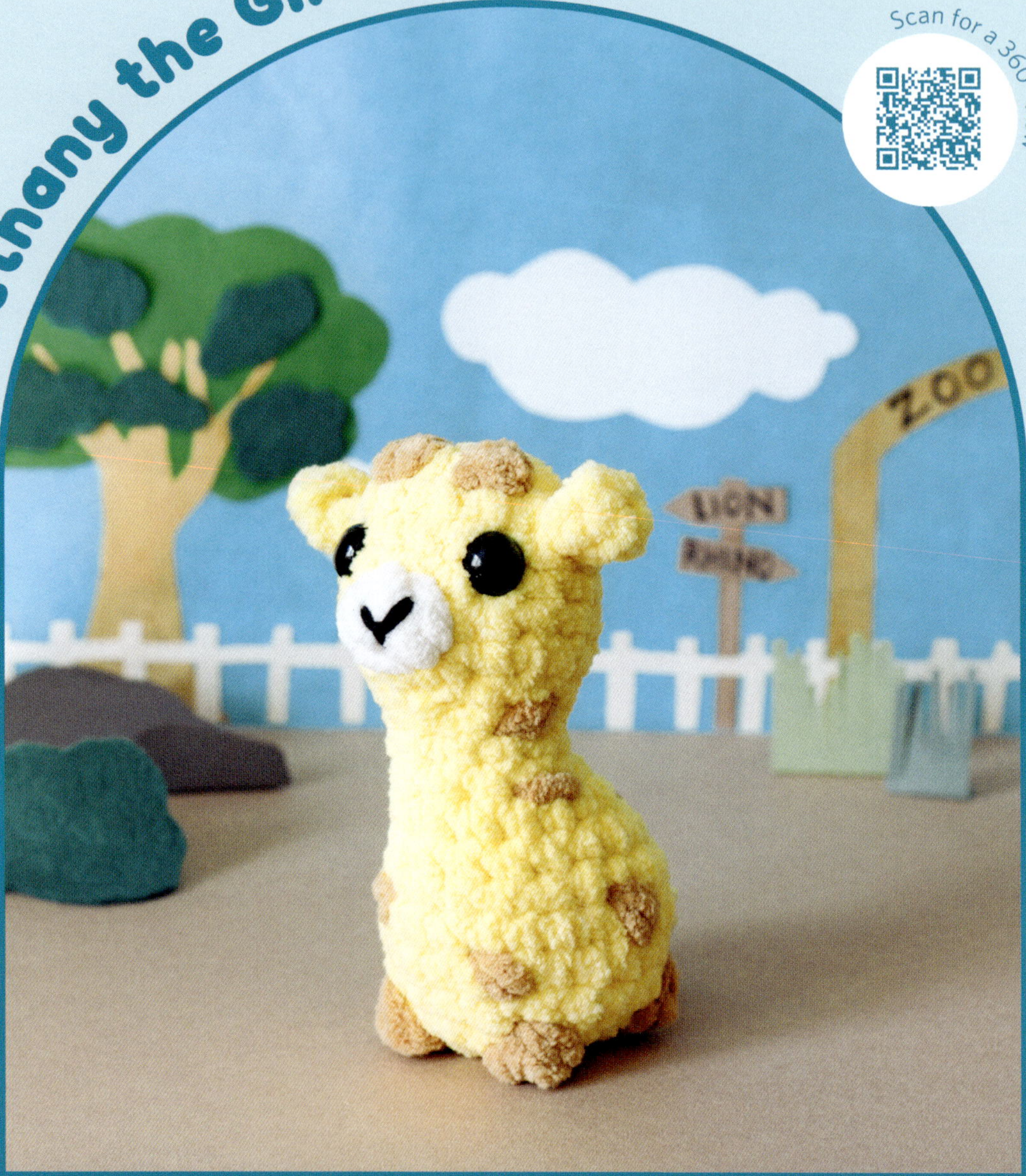

Bethany the Giraffe may be one of the "tall ones," but in this Itty Bitty zoo they're perfectly pocket-sized. They spend their mornings nibbling leaves from the highest twigs, then bending down to share them with friends. Full of gentle grace, Bethany is the quiet guardian of the group.

Bethany might look tall and grand, but don't be daunted: This is actually a very simple pattern. This Itty Bitty design is proof that big-looking shapes can still be quick and easy to make.

Yarn

- Super bulky weight chenille yarn in three colors: yellow, light brown, and warm white
- DK weight cotton yarn in black
- Shown in A Really Good Chenille Yarn by ZaddyCrafts in the colorways Playful (yellow), Gentle (light brown), and Simple (warm white), and Friends Cotton 8/8 by Hobbii in Black

Hook

- 5 mm crochet hook
- Find a full list of notions on page 16, and details for yarn substitutions and hook sizes on page 17.

Special Techniques

- 2dc Bobble Stitch (B2O) (page 38)
- 3dc Bobble Stitch (B3O) (page 39)
- 4dc Bobble Stitch (B4O) (page 40)
- Color Changing Bobble Stitch (CCB2O/CCB3O/CCB4O) (page 41)

Bethany the Giraffe Pattern

Body

Starting with yellow:

Round 1. MC, 6sc. (6)

Round 2. 2inc, CCB2O: light brown, sc in same st, sc, CCB2O: light brown in same st, 2inc. (12)

Round 3. 3sc, ch4, work down the chain starting in the third chain from your hook, hdc, sc, sc into next available st of the body, (inc, sc) x 2, inc, ch4, work down the chain starting in the third chain from your hook, hdc, sc, sc into next available st of the body, 2sc. (15)

Rounds 4-5. sc around. (2 rounds of 15)

Round 6. 7sc, CCB4O: warm white, 7sc. (15)

Round 7. sc around. (15)

Add safety eyes between Rounds 4 and 5 with approximately 4 stitches between the eyes.

Round 8. (sc, dec) x 5. (10)

Rounds 9-10. sc around. (2 rounds of 10)

Start stuffing Bethany the Giraffe and continue stuffing as you go.

Round 11. 2inc, 8sc. (12)

Round 12. 4inc, 8sc. (16)

Round 13. 2sc, 4inc, 10sc. (20)

Round 14. (4sc, inc) x 4. (24)

Round 15. sc around. (24)

Round 16. sc 8, ch3, work down the chain starting in the second chain from your hook, 2slst, sc into the next available st of the body, 15sc. (24)

Round 17. (sc, dec, sc) x 6. (18)

Round 18. 4sc, CCB3O: light brown, 3sc, CCB3O: light brown, 4sc, CCB3O: light brown, 3sc, CCB3O: light brown. (18)

> **Note**: The bobble stitches represent the legs for this Itty Bitty. Due to tension, you may need to adjust their placement so they align properly.

Round 19. 9dec. (9)

Fasten off and close up the remaining stitches.

Spots

Using light brown yarn, embroider small brown spots all over the body by adapting the Making a Line technique on page 56.

Nose

Using black cotton yarn, embroider a small "Y" shape on the warm white B4O from Round 6.

Nice work! Bethany the Giraffe is done! Let's check in on our cheekiest friend, Millie the Monkey.

Millie the Monkey

Full of boundless energy, Millie the Monkey is the zoo's star entertainer, always ready to turn the zoo into their own stage. This Itty Bitty performer leaps dramatically from branch to branch, spinning midair as though the crowd is holding its breath. Every landing comes with a grand pose, a bow, and a wink before they jet off for their next performance.

Millie the Monkey is a fun way to practice color changes while keeping the stitches straightforward. This very charming Itty Bitty project is full of personality and easy to follow.

Yarn

- Super bulky weight chenille yarn in two colors: brown and light brown
- Shown in A Really Good Chenille Yarn by ZaddyCrafts in the colorways Cuddly (brown) and Gentle (light brown)

Hook

- 5 mm crochet hook
- Find a full list of notions on page 16, and details for yarn substitutions and hook sizes on page 17.

Special Techniques

- 2dc Bobble Stitch (B2O) (page 38)
- 3dc Bobble Stitch (B3O) (page 39)
- Color Changing Bobble Stitch (CCB2O/CCB3O) (page 41)
- Half Color Change Single Crochet (HCCsc) (page 48)
- Surface Crochet (page 51)

Millie the Monkey Pattern

Body

Starting with brown:

Round 1. MC, 6sc. (6)

Round 2. 6inc. (12)

Round 3. (sc, inc) x 6. (18)

Round 4. sc around. (18)

Round 5. sc5, CC to light brown, 3sc, HCCsc: pull through a loop of brown followed by pulling a loop of light brown through both loops to complete, 3sc, CC to brown: 6sc. (18)

Rounds 6–7. 5sc, CC to light brown: 7sc, CC to brown: 6sc. (2 rounds of 18)

Round 8. 4sc, inc, CC to light brown: dec, 3sc, dec, CC to brown: inc, 5sc. (18)

Round 9. (sc, dec) x 6. (12)

Add the safety eyes between Rounds 6 and 7, with approximately 4 stitches between the eyes. The HCCsc will line up with the center of the eyes.

Start stuffing Millie the Monkey and continue stuffing as you go.

Round 10. Work in FLO: (sc, inc, sc) x 4. (16)

Round 11. 6sc, CCB2O: light brown, 4sc, CCB2O: light brown, 4sc. (16)

Round 12. sc around. (16)

Round 13. sc, ch7, work down the chain starting with the second loop from the hook: 6slst, sc into the next available sc of the body, 5sc, CCB3O: light brown, 3sc, CCB3O: light brown, 4sc. (16)

Round 14. 8dec. (8)

Fasten off and close up the remaining stitches.

Ears

Using surface crochet, you will create two ears on either side of Millie's head, about 2 stitches away from the eyes. These should span over two rounds and are surface crocheted in a small semi-circle shape.

Attach brown yarn: ch, dcinc, ch, slst into the head.

Fasten off and weave in any yarn tails.

Nose

Using brown yarn, embroider a small nose between the two eyes, and one round of stitches below. This should span across 2 stitches and only loop around twice. Make sure you do a singular loop from the bottom to create a small "T" shape.

Cheeky Millie the Monkey is complete! Let's swing on over to Rhiannon the Rhino next.

Rhiannon the Rhino

Grounded and dependable, Rhiannon the Rhino is the quiet anchor of the zoo crew. This Itty Bitty rhino takes life at their own pace, unhurried and unshaken by the busyness around them. When friends are buzzing with excitement or wrapped up in mischief, Rhiannon is the one who offers a steady presence with a nod or a reassuring nudge, or simply by standing close so you know they're there.

This Itty Bitty is a return to simplicity: Quick, cute, and beginner-friendly, Rhiannon has no surprises and no major learning curves.

Yarn

- Super bulky weight chenille yarn in two colors: light gray and warm white
- Shown in A Really Good Chenille Yarn by ZaddyCrafts in the colorways Charming (light gray) and Simple (warm white)

Hook

- 5 mm crochet hook
- Find a full list of notions on page 16, and details for yarn substitutions and hook sizes on page 17.

Special Techniques

- 3dc Bobble Stitch (B3O) (page 39)
- Color Changing Bobble Stitch (CCB2O) (page 41)
- Multiple Stitches in One Stitch (_in1) (page 47)
- Picot Stitch (PS) (page 43)

Rhiannon the Rhino Pattern

Starting with light gray:

Round 1. MC, 6sc. (6)

Round 2. CCB2O: warm white, inc, (sc, inc) x 2. (9)

Round 3. 3inc, 6sc. (12)

Round 4. 6inc, 6sc. (18)

Round 5. (5sc, inc) x 3. (21)

Round 6. 5sc, PS, 3sc, PS, 5sc, B3O, 3sc, B3O, sc. (21)

Note: The bobble stitches represent the legs for this Itty Bitty. Due to tension, you may need to adjust their placement so they align properly.

Rounds 7-10. sc around. (4 rounds of 21)

Round 11. 16c, B3O, 2sc, B3O, sc. (21)

Add the safety eyes between Rounds 4 and 5, with approximately 4 stitches between the eyes.

Start stuffing Rhiannon the Rhino and continue stuffing as you go.

Round 12. (5sc, dec) x 3. (18)

Round 13. (sc, dec) x 6. (12)

Round 14. 2dec, sc, work in FLO: (sc, hdc, sc)in1, 2dec, sc. (7)

Fasten off the yarn and close up the remaining stitches.

Wow! You charged through Rhiannon the Rhino! Now for the grand finale, the zoo royalty: Dzmitry the Lion.

Dzmitry the Lion

Though pint-sized, Dzmitry the Lion has a heart that fills the whole zoo. They watch every antic with pride, tail swishing in excitement, ears alert for the next daring act. From the giraffe's gentle stretch to the monkey's tumbling flips, Dzmitry cheers them all on with an Itty Bitty rumble that's more comforting than any roar.

A quick, beginner-friendly make with a highlight: the lion's flashy mane. This Itty Bitty project is simple yet striking, perfect for adding flair to your collection.

Yarn

- Super bulky weight chenille yarn in three colors: warm white, light brown, and brown
- DK weight cotton yarn in black
- Shown in A Really Good Chenille Yarn by ZaddyCrafts in the colorways Simple (warm white), Gentle (light brown), and Cuddly (brown), and Friends Cotton 8/8 by Hobbii in Black

Hook

- 5 mm crochet hook
- Find a full list of notions on page 16, and details for yarn substitutions and hook sizes on page 17.

Special Techniques

- 3dc Bobble Stitch (B3O) (page 39)
- Invisible Fasten Off (page 50)
- Picot Stitch (PS) (page 43)

Dzmitry the Lion Pattern

Body

Starting with warm white:

Round 1. MC, 6sc. (6)

Round 2. (sc, inc) x 3. (9)

Round 3. 3inc, CC to light brown: 6sc. (12)

Round 4. 6inc, 6sc. (18)

Round 5. (5sc, inc) x 3. (21)

Round 6. (5sc, PS) x 2, 9sc. (21)

Round 7. CC to brown and work in FLO: 21inc. (42)

Fasten off with an Invisible Fasten Off to the first st of Round 7 and weave in any yarn tails.

Attach light brown yarn to the first unused back loop from Round 7, and continue working in the unused back loops from Round 7 in the next round.

Round 8. 16sc, B3O, 3sc, B3O. (21)

> **Note:** The bobble stitches represent the legs for this Itty Bitty. Due to tension, you may need to adjust their placement so they align properly.

Round 9. 5sc, 3dec, 10sc. (18)

Rounds 10–12. sc around. (3 rounds of 18)

Round 13. 14sc, B3O, 2sc, B3O. (18)

Add the safety eyes between Rounds 4 and 5, with approximately 4 stitches between the eyes.

Start stuffing Dzmitry the Lion and continue stuffing as you go.

Round 14. (sc, dec) x 6. (12)

Round 15. 3dec, sc, ch6, work down the chain starting in the second loop from the hook: 5slst, sc into the next available st of the body, 2dec. (7)

Fasten off the yarn and close up the remaining stitches.

Nose

Using black cotton yarn, embroider a small nose on the end of the snout. This should span across 2 stitches and only loop around twice. Make sure you do a singular loop from the bottom, pulling it softly to create a small "Y" shape.

Roar-some! Dzmitry the Lion rounds off our Day at the Zoo—what a wild ride that was! Let's cool down the excitement and head somewhere that's quite literally a little bit cooler.

Frozen Wonderlands

Step into the Frozen Wonderlands, a little world crafted from snow, ice, and laughter. Here, the winds whisper softly, and the crunch of tiny steps is enough to bring the quiet landscape to life. In this Itty Bitty Arctic, warmth isn't found in the weather, but in the joy of friendship.

Terrance the Seal (page 102) loves slipping and sliding across the ice, showing off playful dives that always earn cheers from the others. Not far behind, Aaron the Snow Hare (page 100) bounds swiftly across drifts, keeping the group laughing with their quick, darting hops. Watching over the scene is the gentle giant, Kevin the Polar Bear (page 104), a calm and steady leader who makes everyone feel safe. Out at sea, Henry the Humpback Whale (page 106) surfaces with a song, their voice carrying across the ice like a mini concert for the whole crew. And waddling determinedly in line, Willy the Baby Penguin (page 98) brings joy and endless giggles with every tumble. Together, this frosty family turns even the chilliest days into a celebration of friendship.

Willy the Baby Penguin

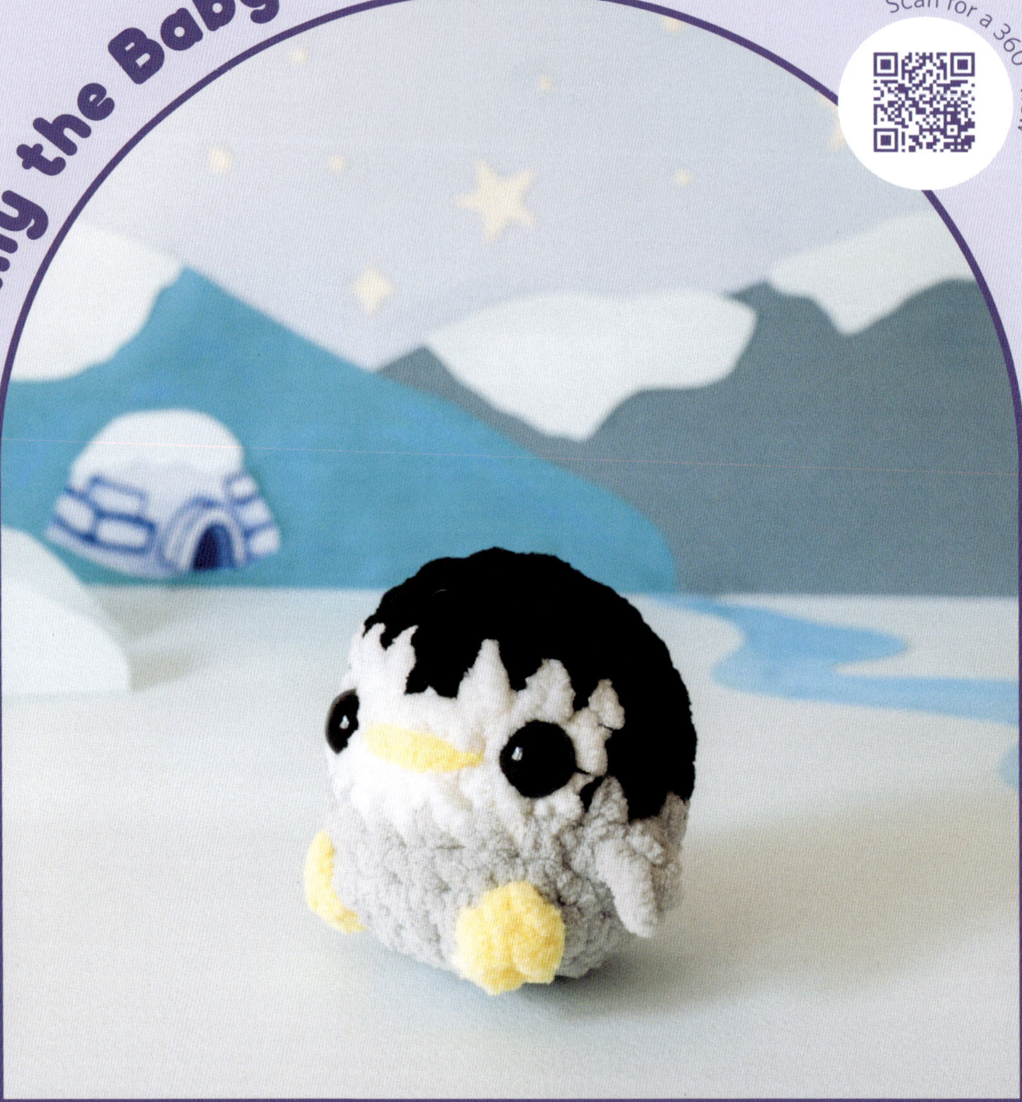

Willy the Baby Penguin is not only small, but they're endlessly curious about the big frozen world around them. This Itty Bitty penguin waddles after their friends trying to copy their every move: hopping after the snow hare, humming along with the whale's songs, and attempting to match the polar bear's grand stride. Their tumbles and stumbles are part of their charm, proving that even the tiniest steps can be full of heart.

A playful design for color change practice, similar to Aspen the Owl (page 76), Willy can be a fun way to practice your essential amigurumi skills while learning newer special techniques.

Yarn

- Super bulky weight chenille yarn in four colors: black, warm white, light gray, and yellow
- Shown in A Really Good Chenille Yarn by ZaddyCrafts in the colorways Mischief (black), Simple (warm white), Charming (light gray), and Playful (yellow)

Hook

- 5 mm crochet hook
- Find a full list of notions on page 16, and details for yarn substitutions and hook sizes on page 17.

Special Techniques

- 2dc Bobble Stitch (B2O) (page 38)
- Color Changing Bobble Stitch (CCB2O) (page 41)
- Half Color Change Single Crochet (HCCsc) (page 48)
- Picot Stitch (PS) (page 43)

Willy the Baby Penguin Pattern

Body

Starting with black:

Round 1. MC, 6sc. (6)

Round 2. 6inc. (12)

Round 3. (sc, inc) x 6. (18)

Round 4. sc around. (18)

Round 5. sc5, CC to warm white, 3sc, HCCsc: pull through a loop of black followed by pulling a loop of warm white through both loops to complete, 3sc, CC to black: 6sc. (18)

Round 6. CC to light gray, slst, 4sc, CC to warm white: 7sc, CC to light gray: 6sc. (18)

Round 7. Work in BLO: sc, work in both loops: 3sc, PS, CC to warm white: 7sc, CC to light gray: sc, PS, 4sc. (18)

Rounds 8-9. sc around. (2 rounds of 18)

Round 10. 6sc, CCB2O: yellow, 4sc, CCB2O: yellow, 6sc. (18)

Note: The bobble stitches represent the feet for this Itty Bitty. Due to tension, you may need to adjust their placement so they align properly.

Add the safety eyes between Rounds 6 and 7, with approximately 4 stitches between the eyes. The HCCsc will line up with the centers of the eyes.

Start stuffing Willy the Baby Penguin and continue stuffing as you go.

Round 11. (sc, dec) x 6. (12)

Round 12. 6dec. (6)

Fasten off and close up the remaining stitches.

Beak

With yellow yarn, embroider a small beak between the two eyes, between Rounds 6 and 7. This should span across 2 stitches and only loop around twice.

Chilly Willy is finished! Waddle on over to check out Aaron the Snow Hare next.

Aaron the Snow Hare

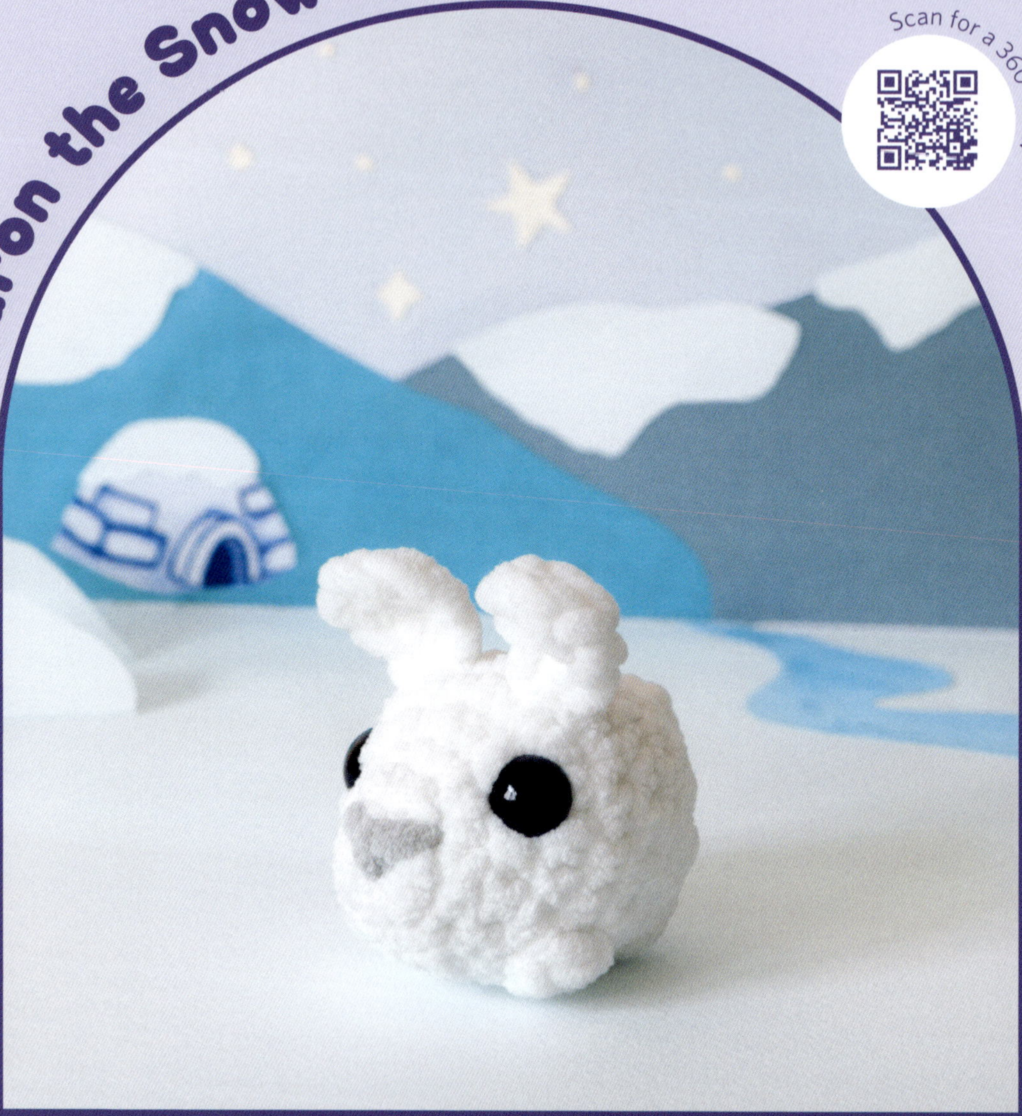

With ears perked high and paws always ready to spring forward, Aaron the Snow Hare embodies the essence of adventure. Small but unstoppable, they zigzag through the drifts with boundless energy, pausing just long enough to wiggle their nose before zooming off again. To them, the Arctic is less a frozen land and more a playground bursting with possibility.

Aaron is one of the quickest and simplest designs in this chapter, an easy mini pattern that's perfect for beginners. Try experimenting with colors to create hares from all over the world.

Yarn

- Super bulky weight chenille yarn in two colors: cool white and light gray
- Shown in A Really Good Chenille Yarn by ZaddyCrafts in the colorways Basic (cool white) and Charming (light gray)

Hook

- 5 mm crochet hook
- Find a full list of notions on page 16, and details for yarn substitutions and hook sizes on page 17.

Special Techniques

- 2dc Bobble Stitch (B2O) (page 38)
- 4dc Bobble Stitch (B4O) (page 40)

Aaron the Snow Hare Pattern

Body

Starting with cool white:

Round 1. MC, 6sc. (6)

Round 2. (sc, inc) x 3. (9)

Round 3. 3inc, 6sc. (12)

Round 4. 6inc, 6sc. (18)

Round 5. 5sc, ch5, work down the ch starting in the third loop from the hook: dc, hdc, sc, sc into the next available st of the body, 2sc, ch5, work down the ch starting in the third loop from the hook: dc, hdc, sc, sc into the next available st of the body, 4sc, B2O, 3sc, B2O. (18)

Note: The bobble stitches represent the legs for this Itty Bitty. Due to tension, you may need to adjust their placement so they align properly.

Rounds 6–8. sc around. (3 rounds of 18)

Add the safety eyes between Rounds 4 and 5, with approximately 4 stitches between the eyes.

Start stuffing Aaron the Snow Hare and continue stuffing as you go.

Round 9. 14sc, B2O, 2sc, B2O. (18)

Round 10. (sc, dec) x 6. (12)

Round 11. dec, sc, dec, B4O, (dec, sc) x 2. (8)

Fasten off the yarn and close up the remaining stitches.

Nose

Using light gray yarn, embroider a small nose between the two eyes. This should span across 2 stitches and only loop around twice. Make sure you do a singular loop from the bottom, pulling it softly to create a small "Y" shape.

Snow much fun! Aaron the Snow Hare is done! Terrance the Seal awaits by the ice.

Terrance the Seal

Terrance the Seal is the jolliest soul in the Arctic. They may be Itty Bitty in size, but this seal has an overflowing essence of optimism. They love sliding belly-first down frosty slopes and popping up with a squeak of laughter as their friends cheer them on. Whenever the group needs a dose of joy, Terrance the Seal is always there to lift the mood.

Cute, simple, and unique, Terrance is a well-rounded design that's fun to crochet and full of personality.

Yarn

- Super bulky weight chenille yarn in two colors: light gray and warm white
- DK weight cotton yarn in black
- Shown in A Really Good Chenille Yarn by ZaddyCrafts in the colorways Charming (light gray) and Simple (warm white), and Friends Cotton 8/8 by Hobbii in Black

Hook

- 5 mm crochet hook
- Find a full list of notions on page 16, and details for yarn substitutions and hook sizes on page 17.

Special Techniques

- 4dc Bobble Stitch (B4O) (page 40)
- Color Changing Bobble Stitch (CCB4O) (page 41)
- Single Crochet Three Together (sc3tog) (page 49)

Terrance the Seal Pattern

Body

Starting with light gray:

Round 1. MC, 6sc. (6)

Round 2. 6inc. (12)

Round 3. (sc, inc, sc) x 4. (16)

Rounds 4–5. sc around. (2 rounds of 16)

Round 6. 9sc, (CCB4O: warm white) x 2, 5sc. (16)

Round 7. sc around. (16)

Round 8. 2inc, sc, 2inc, sc11. (20)

Round 9. 2sc, 2inc, sc, 2inc, sc13. (24)

Add the safety eyes between Rounds 4 and 5, with approximately 3 stitches between the eyes.

Start stuffing Terrance the Seal and continue stuffing as you go.

Round 10. 15sc, ch4, work back down the ch starting in the second loop: 3sc, sc into next st of the body, 7sc, ch4, work back down the ch starting in the second loop: 3sc, sc into next available st of the body. (24)

Round 11. 8sc, ch5, work down the ch starting in the third loop from the hook: dc, hdc, sc, sc into the base of the ch, ch5, work down the ch starting in the third loop from the hook: dc, hdc, sc, sc into the next available st of the body, 15sc. (25)

Round 12. (dec, sc) x 2, sc3tog, sc, (dec, sc) x 5. (18)

Round 13. 8dec. (8)

Fasten off the yarn and close up the remaining stitches.

Nose

Using black yarn, embroider a small nose between the two bobble stitches on Round 6. This should span across 2 stitches and only loop around twice. Make sure you do a singular loop from in between the bobble stitches, pulling it softly to create a small "Y" shape.

You have truly sealed the deal with this one! Next up, Kevin the Polar Bear.

Kevin the Polar Bear

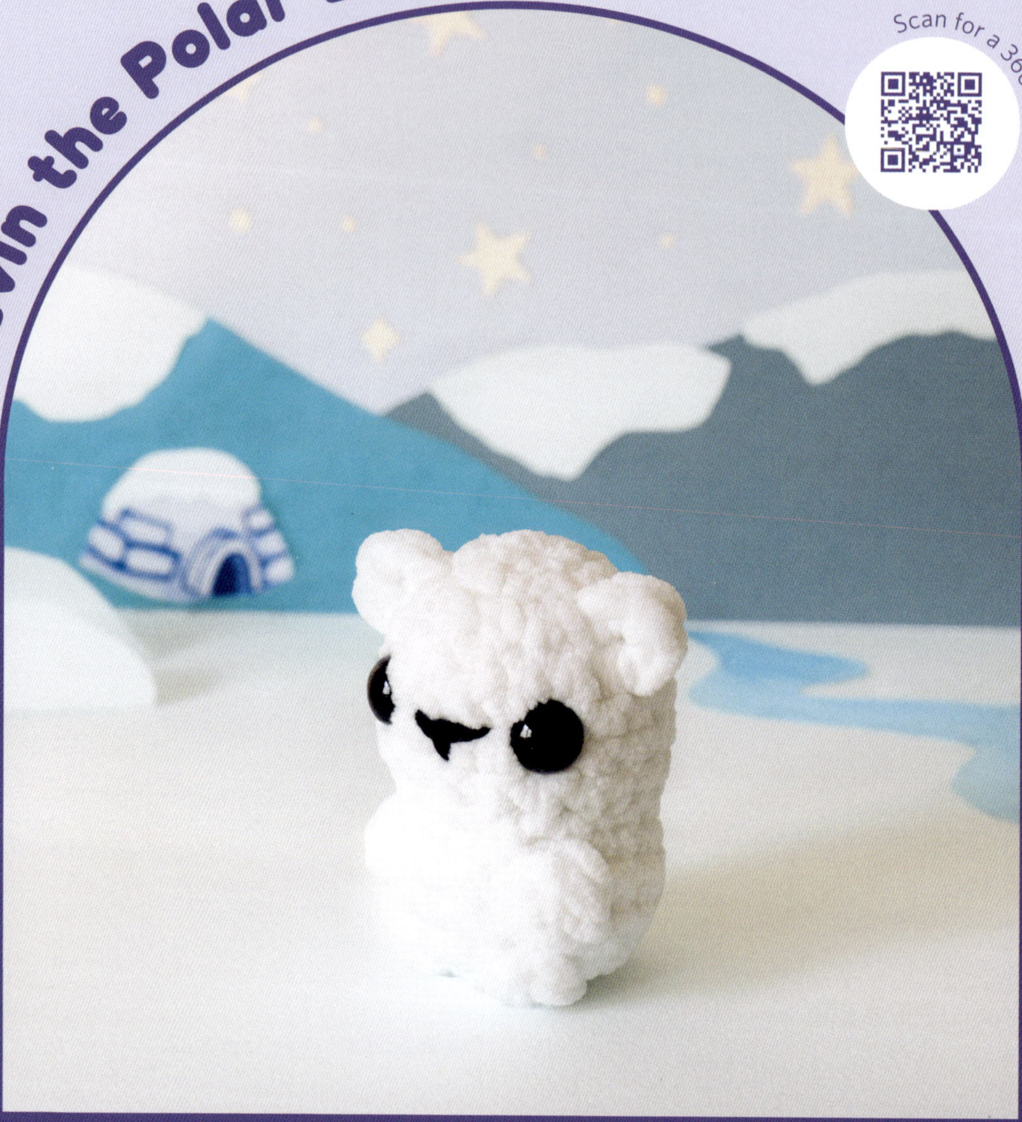

Steady and protective with the biggest heart, Kevin the Polar Bear is the fatherly figure of the group. They're strong and dependable, and their heart truly shines brightest when they're helping others, whether they're gently guiding the baby penguin over icy patches or letting the hare climb onto their back for a ride. Their presence keeps everyone feeling safe and looked after in this Itty Bitty world.

Much like Aaron the Snow Hare (page 100), Kevin is a classic, beginner-friendly pattern that's simple, satisfying, and very versatile. Try swapping in different colors to create your own unique bears.

Yarn

- Super bulky weight chenille yarn in cool white
- DK weight cotton yarn in black
- Shown in A Really Good Chenille Yarn by ZaddyCrafts in the colorway Basic (cool white) and Friends Cotton 8/8 by Hobbii in Black

Hook

- 5 mm crochet hook
- Find a full list of notions on page 16, and details for yarn substitutions and hook sizes on page 17.

Special Techniques

- 2dc Bobble Stitch (B2O) (page 38)
- 3dc Bobble Stitch (B3O) (page 39)
- Surface Crochet (page 51)

Kevin the Polar Bear Pattern

Body

Starting with cool white:

Round 1. MC, 6sc. (6)

Round 2. 6inc. (12)

Round 3. (sc, inc) x 6. (18)

Rounds 4–7. sc around. (4 rounds of 18)

Round 8. (sc, dec) x 6. (12)

Round 9. Work in FLO: (sc, inc, sc) x 4. (16)

Round 10. 6sc, B2O, 4sc, B2O, 4sc. (16)

> **Note:** The bobble stitches represent the arms and legs for this Itty Bitty. Due to tension, you may need to adjust their placement so they align properly.

Add the safety eyes between Rounds 5 and 6, with approximately 4 stitches between the eyes. The bobble stitches from Round 10 should line up so they look like they are approximately one st out from the eyes.

Start stuffing Kevin the Polar Bear and continue stuffing as you go.

Round 11. sc around. (16)

Round 12. 7sc, B3O, 3sc, B3O, 4sc. (16)

Round 13. 8dec. (8)

Fasten off the yarn and close up the remaining stitches.

Ears

Using surface crochet, you will create two ears on either side of Kevin's head. These should span over Rounds 3 and 4 and are crocheted in small semi-circle shapes.

For each ear, attach cool white yarn between Rounds 4 and 5: ch1, hdcinc into a diagonal stitch moving away from the eyes and one round above, ch1, slst into the stitch that is between Rounds 2 and 3 and a stitch moving closer to the eyes.

Fasten off and weave in any yarn tails.

Nose

Using black yarn, embroider a small nose between the two eyes. This should span across 2 stitches and only loop around twice. Make sure you do a singular loop from the bottom, pulling it softly to create a small "Y" shape.

Bear-illiant! Kevin is done. Let's take a quick dip to visit Henry the Humpback Whale.

Henry the Humpback Whale

Although small, Henry the Humpback Whale is the grand voice of the Frozen Wonderlands, filling the waters with songs that can be heard for miles. Each note feels like it carries a story, deep, powerful, and full of emotion. When they rise to the surface, it's as if they're stepping into a spotlight, ready to share their next encore with the world.

Quick, fuss-free, and charming, Henry is a simple, low-effort pattern that makes a big splash.

Yarn

- Super bulky weight chenille yarn in two colors: blue and warm white
- Shown in A Really Good Chenille Yarn by ZaddyCrafts in the colorways Adventurous (blue) and Simple (warm white)

Hook

- 5 mm crochet hook
- Find a full list of notions on page 16, and details for yarn substitutions and hook sizes on page 17.

Special Techniques

- Multiple Stitches in One Stitch (_in1) (page 47)
- Single Crochet Three Together (sc3tog) (page 49)

Henry the Humpback Whale Pattern

Starting with blue:

Round 1. ch6. (6)

Round 2. Work down the ch starting in the second loop from the hook: 4sc, 3scin1, turn your work and continue working into the other side of your initial ch: 4sc, 3scin1. (14)

Round 3. (4sc, inc, sc, inc) x 2. (18)

Round 4. (4sc, inc, sc, inc, sc, inc) x 2. (24)

Rounds 5–6. sc around. (2 rounds of 24)

Round 7. 3sc, ch3, work back down the ch starting in the second loop from the hook:

2sc, sc into next available st of the body, 11sc, ch3, work back down the ch starting in the second loop from the hook: 2sc, sc into next available st of the body, 5sc, ch3, work back down the ch starting in the second loop from the hook: 2sc, sc into the base of the last sc in the body, ch3, work back down the ch starting in the second loop from the hook: 2sc, sc into next available st of the body x 2, CC to warm white: slst, sc. (25)

Complete 1 sc, and move your stitch marker to this st. This is now your new end of round. Continue as normal.

Round 8. 4sc, work in BLO: dec, (sc, dec) x 2, work in both loops: 4sc, dec, sc, sc3tog, sc, dec. (18)

Add the safety eyes between Rounds 6 and 7, with approximately 7 stitches between the eyes. These eyes should line up with each end of the line of BLO from Round 7.

Stuff Henry the Humpback Whale and continue stuffing as you go.

Round 9. 4sc, dec, sc, dec, 4sc, dec, sc, dec. (14)

Round 10. 7dec. (7)

Fasten off the yarn and close up the remaining stitches.

Whale done! Henry wraps up your Frozen Wonderland crew. Where to next? Warmer waters?

Tropical Treasures

Welcome to the sparkling shallows and vibrant reefs of the tropics, where life moves with the rhythm of the waves. In this chapter, you'll discover creatures who shimmer, glide, and scuttle through a sun-soaked paradise. Every corner of the reef holds its own tiny wonder, making it a small world both colorful and calm.

Juniper the Jellyfish (page 112) drifts like a floating lantern, casting a gentle glow as they pulse through the water. Nearby, Chris the Crab (page 114) is busy defending their favorite sandy hideout, waving claws dramatically at anyone who dares to peek. Hege the Seahorse (page 116) sways with the current, a quiet dreamer wrapped around coral stems. Meanwhile, Brooke the Fish (page 118) darts in shimmering schools, always quick to chase a sparkle. And then there's Thanh the Turtle (page 110), the most relaxed of them all, content to bask in a patch of sunlight or float lazily with the tide, reminding everyone that sometimes the best adventures are the slow ones.

Thanh the Turtle

Thanh the Turtle is the reef's friendly homebody, happiest when tucked into their favorite patch of coral. They love familiar routines, whether they're drifting lazily in the reef, greeting friends as they pass, or watching the bustle from their cozy corner. Small and steady, Thanh may not go looking for adventure, but they're always glad when their friends come back to share stories.

One of the cutest designs in the book, Thanh features an interesting join technique that creates charming results. This is a sweet Itty Bitty make that feels as rewarding as it looks.

Yarn

- Super bulky weight chenille yarn in two colors: light brown and green
- Shown in A Really Good Chenille Yarn by ZaddyCrafts in the colorways Gentle (light brown) and Witty (green)

Hook

- 5 mm crochet hook
- Find a full list of notions on page 16, and details for yarn substitutions and hook sizes on page 17.

Special Techniques

- 3dc Bobble Stitch (B3O) (page 39)

Thanh the Turtle Pattern

Head

Starting with light brown:

Round 1. MC, 6sc. (6)

Round 2. 6inc. (12)

Round 3. (sc, inc) x 6. (18)

Rounds 4–7. sc around. (4 rounds of 18)

Round 8. 9dec. (9)

Add safety eyes between Rounds 5 and 6 about 3 stitches apart and stuff the head. You do not need to stuff any further down the neck as we make it. If you want more control of which way Thanh the Turtle's head is facing, I suggest waiting until you've completed round 11, then pinching the open end together. This edge will show you where the head attaches to the body so you can plan your eye placement accordingly.

Round 9. (sc, dec) x 3. (6)

Rounds 10–11. sc around. (2 rounds of 6)

Round 12. Flatten the piece and sc across 2 stitches at a time. (3)

Fasten off and weave in any yarn tails.

Shell

Starting with green:

Round 1. MC, 6sc. (6)

Round 2. 6inc. (12)

Round 3. (sc, inc) x 6. (18)

Rounds 4–5. sc around. (2 rounds of 18)

Round 6. Work in FLO: sc around. (18)

Round 7. CC to light brown and work in the leftover back loops from Round 5: join the head by completing 3sc through the last row of the head and the next 3 stitches of the body, sc, (B3O, 3sc) x 3, B3O, sc. (18)

> **Note**: The bobble stitches represent the legs for this Itty Bitty. Due to tension, you may need to adjust their placement so they align properly.

Start stuffing the shell and continue stuffing as you go. Consider stuffing the shell with something weighted, such as weighted beads, so that Thanh the Turtle stays upright.

Round 8. 9dec. (9)

Fasten off, leaving a long yarn tail for sewing.

Close up the piece and insert the rest of the yarn tail through the body. Use this yarn tail to fasten the head up onto the shell, so the head stays upright.

Slow and steady Thanh is done! Next, glide over to Juniper the Jellyfish.

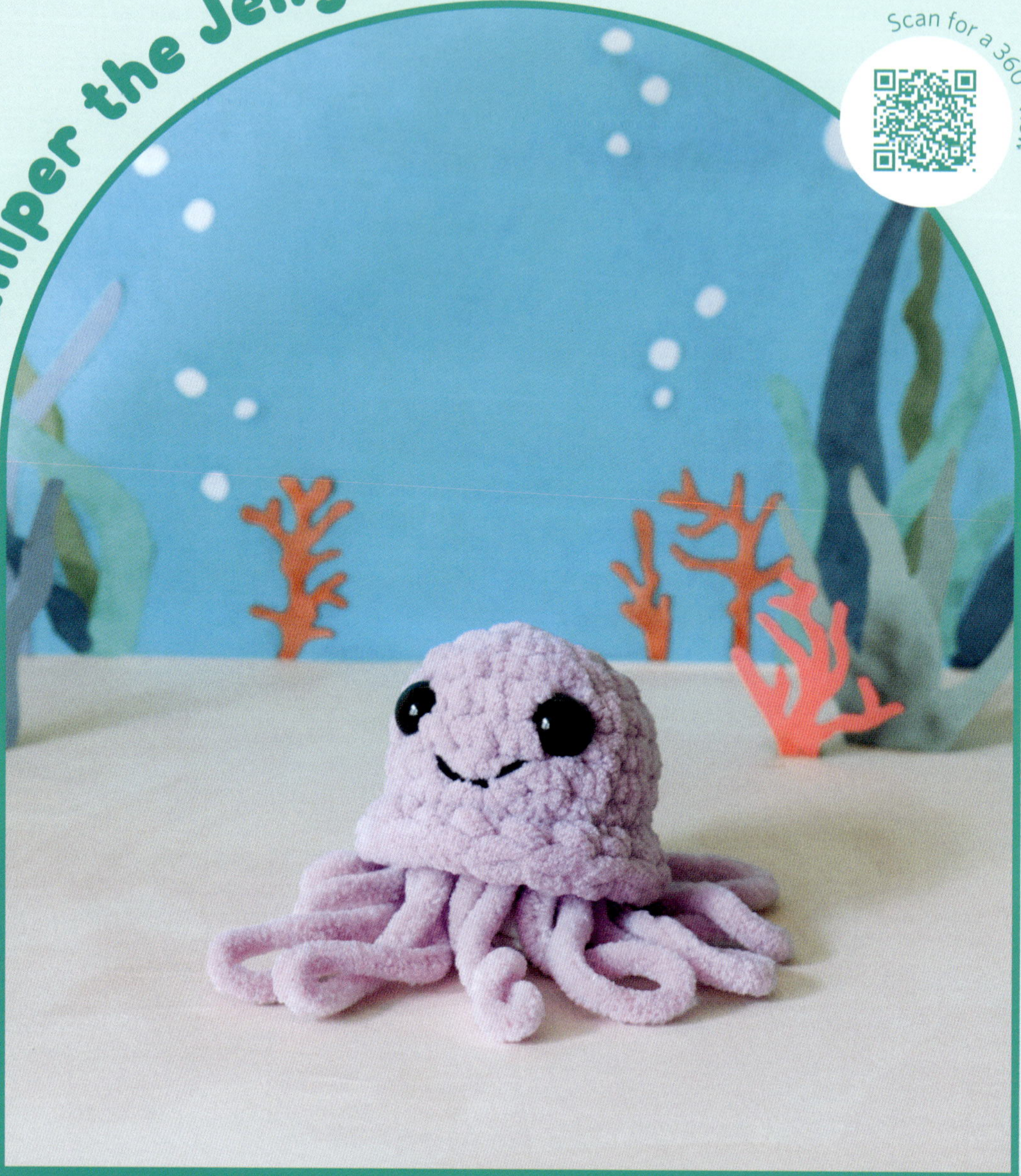

Juniper the Jellyfish is a dancer at heart, floating through the reef as if the whole ocean is their dance floor. They are often lost in daydreams, moving along with the tide while humming little tunes. This small, whimsical jellyfish is less a critter and more a pocket-sized fairy of the sea.

With a unique technique that makes them quick to complete, Juniper is a favorite among crocheters, a fast and satisfying Itty Bitty project that's as dreamy as the jellyfish itself.

Yarn

- Super bulky weight chenille yarn in light purple
- DK weight cotton yarn in black
- Shown in A Really Good Chenille Yarn by ZaddyCrafts in the colorway Whimsy (light purple) and Friends Cotton 8/8 by Hobbii in Black

Hook

- 5 mm crochet hook
- Find a full list of notions on page 16, and details for yarn substitutions and hook sizes on page 17.

Special Techniques

- Invisible Fasten Off (page 50)
- Loop Stitch (loop) (page 46)

Juniper the Jellyfish Pattern

Body

Starting with light purple:

Round 1. MC, 6sc. (6)

Round 2. 6inc. (12)

Round 3. (sc, inc) x 6. (18)

Rounds 4–7. sc around. (4 rounds of 18)

Round 8. Work in FLO: hdc around. (18)

Fasten off with an Invisible Fasten Off into the first st of Round 8 and weave in any yarn tails.

Add the safety eyes between Rounds 4 and 5, with approximately 4 stitches between the eyes.

Start stuffing Juniper the Jellyfish and continue stuffing as you go.

Reattach yarn to the first unused back loop from Round 8.

Round 9. Work in unused back loops only: (sc, loop) x 9. (18)

Round 10. 9dec. (9)

Fasten off and close up the remaining stitches.

Mouth

Using black cotton yarn, embroider a small mouth just below the middle of the two eyes following the Making a Line technique on page 56.

Jelly-tastic! Juniper is finished! Time to float on over to Chris the Crab.

Chris the Crab

Chris the Crab scuttles through the reef like a pint-sized treasure hunter. Every pebble, shell, and coral fragment becomes part of their growing collection, neatly tucked away in their sandy hideout. To Chris, each little find is a story, and their greatest joy is sharing those tiny treasures with friends.

This design is one of our most unique Itty Bitties. Try making Chris the Crab in a range of colors for endless variety. They're one of several tropical patterns that let you play with creative color palettes on an Itty Bitty scale.

Yarn

- Super bulky weight chenille yarn in orange
- Shown in A Really Good Chenille Yarn by ZaddyCrafts in the colorway Charisma (orange)

Hook

- 5 mm crochet hook
- Find a full list of notions on page 16, and details for yarn substitutions and hook sizes on page 17.

Special Techniques

- Invisible Fasten Off (page 50)
- Picot Stitch (PS) (page 43)

Chris the Crab Pattern

Starting with orange:

Round 1. MC, 8sc. (8)

Round 2. 8inc. (16)

Round 3. (3sc, inc) x 4. (20)

Round 4. sc around. (20)

Round 5. Work in FLO: sc around. (20)

Fasten off with an Invisible Fasten Off into the first st of Round 5 and weave in any yarn tails.

Attach orange yarn to the first unused back loop from Round 5.

Round 6. Work in the unused back loops from Round 5: 3sc, 3PS, ch5, work down the ch starting in the third loop from your hook: slst, ch2, work down the ch starting in the third loop from your hook (the same loop as before): slst, 2slst, sc into the next available back loop of the body, 6sc, ch5, work down the ch starting in the third loop from your hook: slst, ch2, work down the ch starting in the third loop from your hook (the same loop as before): slst, 2slst, sc into the next available back loop of the body, 3PS, 3sc. (20)

Attach safety eyes between Rounds 3 and 4 with approximately 4 stitches between them. These should line up with the two pincers made in Round 6 respectively. Start stuffing Chris the Crab and continue stuffing as you go.

Round 7. (3sc, dec) x 4. (16)

Round 8. 8dec. (8)

Fasten off and close up the remaining stitches.

Clawsome! Chris the Crab is complete! Hege the Seahorse is next.

Hege the Seahorse

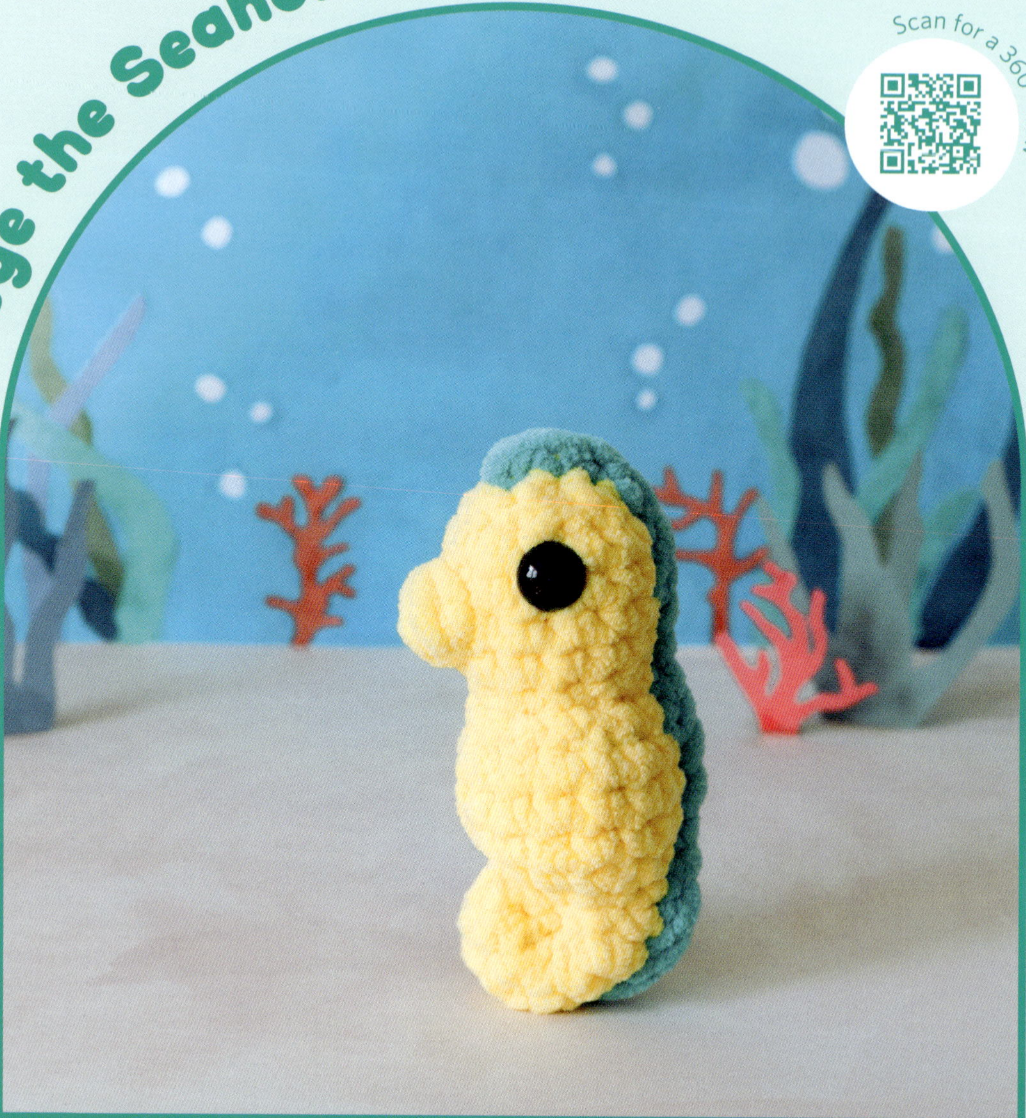

Hege has a soft, sentimental side. They believe the ocean is full of love stories, big and small, and sometimes tease Thanh the Turtle (page 110) that they'll be the star of the next one. Small but full of feeling, Hege is the reef's romantic dreamer.

Hege uses an interesting construction technique—nothing too tricky for a beginner crocheter, just a fun new way to build shapes. They're a colorful Itty Bitty project that is perfect for experimenting with different color palettes.

Yarn

- Super bulky weight chenille yarn in two colors: yellow and turquoise
- Shown in A Really Good Chenille Yarn by ZaddyCrafts in the colorways Playful (yellow) and Intuitive (turquoise)

Hook

- 5 mm crochet hook
- Find a full list of notions on page 16, and details for yarn substitutions and hook sizes on page 17.

Special Techniques

- 4dc Bobble Stitch (B4O) (page 40)
- Surface Crochet (page 51)

Hege the Seahorse Pattern

Body

Starting with yellow:

Round 1. MC, 6sc. (6)

Rounds 2–5. sc around. (4 rounds of 6)

Round 6. sc, tightly roll the piece so that Round 5 is now adjacent to Round 2. Directly surface crochet 2sc into the middle of Row 2. sc back into the 4 st from Round 5, 2sc. (6)

Scan for a video tutorial!

You will now continue to crochet in the round using the 2 stitches from the surface crochet in Round 7.

Round 7. 4inc, 2sc. (10)

Round 8. sc, (inc, sc, inc) x 2, 3sc. (14)

Rounds 9–11. sc around. (3 rounds of 14)

Round 12. 2sc, 5dec, 2sc. (9)

Start stuffing Hege the Seahorse and continue stuffing as you go. You do not need to stuff the curled tail.

Round 13. Work in FLO: (sc, inc, sc) x 3. (12)

Round 14. sc around. (12)

Round 15. 6sc, B4O, 5sc. (12)

Note: The bobble stitch represents the nose on this Itty Bitty. Due to tension, you may need to adjust the placement so it aligns properly.

Rounds 16–17. sc around. (2 rounds of 12)

Round 18. 6dec. (6)

Attach safety eyes between Rounds 16 and 17, with approximately 4 stitches between them. The 4dc bobble stitch from Round 15 should be one round below the middle of these eyes.

Fasten off and close up the remaining stitches.

Fin

Using turquoise yarn, surface crochet a line of sc starting from the top of Hege's head all the way down to their tail curl. This should be in a straight line going down Hege's back. Fasten off and weave in any yarn tails.

Sea-sational! Hege is done, I think I saw a glimmer of Brooke the Fish swimming nearby. Let's check it out!

Brooke the Fish

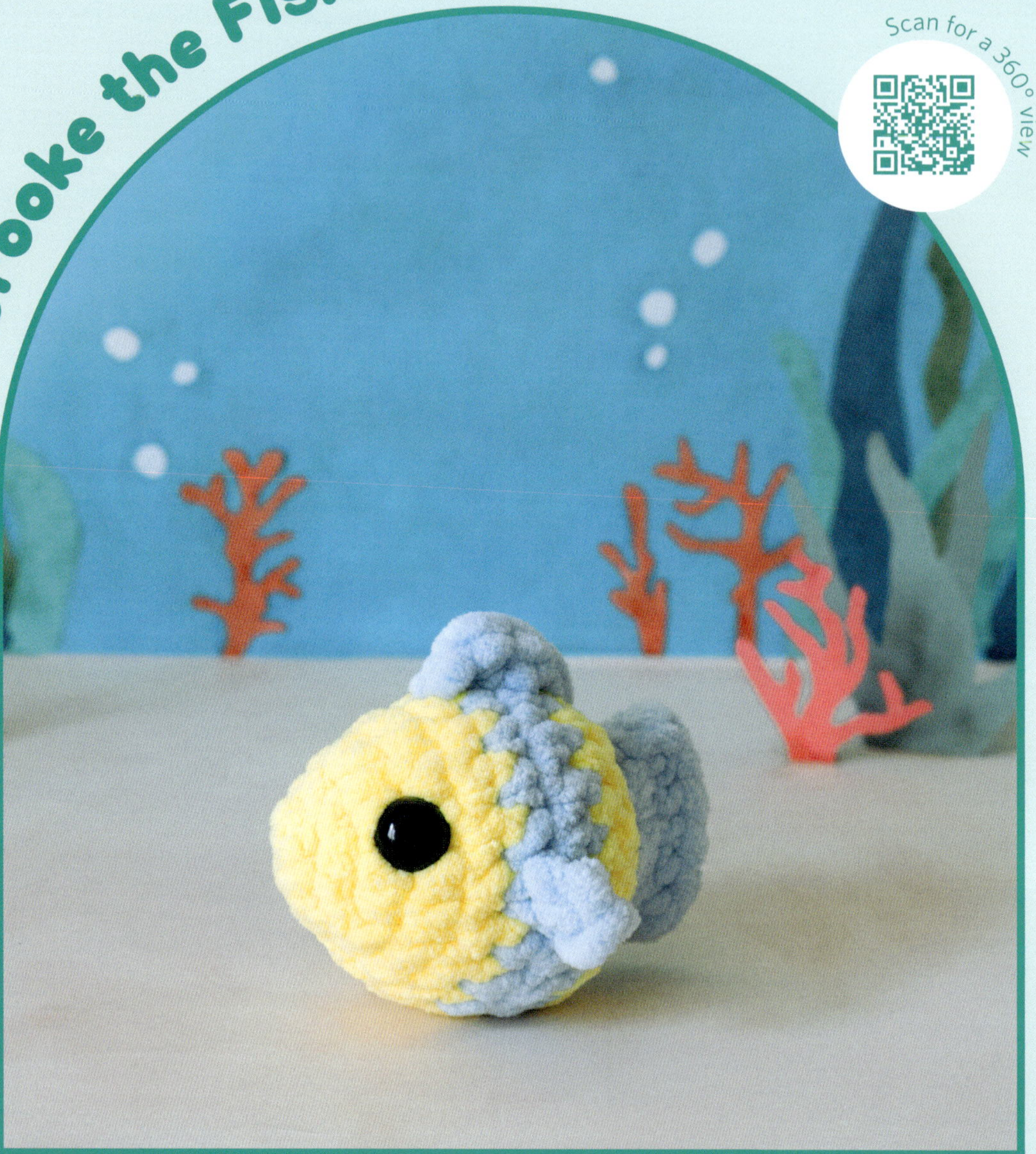

Brooke the Fish is the life of the reef, always darting here, there, and everywhere. Tiny and restless, Brooke loves chasing glimmers of light or weaving through kelp and coral alike, just to see what's hiding around each corner. They're also the chatterbox of the reef, bubbling on about their latest discoveries to anyone who will listen.

The simplest of the tropical patterns, Brooke is a quick and easy Itty Bitty design, perfect for when you want a fast finish with plenty of personality.

Yarn

- Super bulky weight chenille yarn in two colors: yellow and light blue
- Shown in A Really Good Chenille Yarn by ZaddyCrafts in the colorways Playful (yellow) and Spirited (light blue).

Hook

- 5 mm crochet hook
- Find a full list of notions on page 16, and details for yarn substitutions and hook sizes on page 17.

Special Techniques

- Surface Crochet (page 51)

Brooke the Fish Pattern

Body

Starting with yellow:

Round 1. MC, 6sc. (6)

Round 2. (sc, inc) x 3. (9)

Round 3. 9inc. (18)

Rounds 4-5. sc around. (2 rounds of 18)

Round 6. CC to light blue: 4sc, ch2, work back down the ch starting in the second loop from the hook: sc, slst into the base of the fin, sc into next available st of the body, 9sc, ch2, work back down the ch starting in the second loop from the hook: sc, slst into the base of the fin, sc into next available st of the body, 3sc. (18)

In the next round, do not crochet into the slip stitches from Round 6.

Round 7. sc around. (18)

Round 8. CC to yellow: sc around. (18)

Round 9. sc around. (18)

Add the safety eyes between Rounds 3 and 4, with approximately 5 stitches between the eyes. The color changes should be on Brooke's underside.

Start stuffing Brooke the Fish and continue stuffing as you go.

Round 10. (sc, dec) x 6. (12)

Round 11. CC to light blue: 6dec. (6)

Round 12. 6inc. (12)

Round 13. sc, flatten the piece and sc across. Every sc will go across 2 stitches including the first sc from this round. (6)

Fasten off the yarn and close up the remaining stitches.

Top Fin

Using light blue yarn, surface crochet a fin on the top of your fish. The fin will line up with the back fin and the middle of the eyes.

Attach your yarn between Rounds 5 and 6, ch2, hdc in same st, work back down towards the tail fin: hdc, sc, slst into the body and fasten off, weaving in any yarn tails.

You reeled in a winner here! Chapter complete and treasures all found. Let's dry off somewhere new!

Desert Beauties

Welcome to the Itty Bitty desert, where the golden sands may shimmer in the heat but the true magic lives in the small details. Look closer and you'll find a lively crew tucked among the dunes. From prickly plants with warm hearts to creatures of the night with a flair for the dramatic, this little stretch of sand is bursting with personality.

Lisa the Lizard (page 130) darts quickly across the hot sand, pausing only long enough to bask on a sun-warmed stone before skittering off again, while Jake the Snake (page 126) follows along with smooth curiosity. Nearby, Kelsea the Cactus (page 122) greets everyone with cheerful enthusiasm despite their prickly exterior. Scott the Scorpion (page 124) makes a grand entrance, waving pincers and flicking their tail with dramatic flair, and Cameron the Baby Camel (page 128) plods along calmly, steady and unbothered.

Kelsea the Cactus

Bright and bubbly, Kelsea the Cactus is the most unlikely social butterfly. Always eager to welcome friends with a cheerful wave, they insist that their prickles don't mean a thing when it comes to giving out "cactus cuddles." Somehow, this little cactus's shade has become the desert's favorite gathering spot, proof that even the smallest friend can bring the most joy.

Yarn

- Super bulky weight chenille yarn in four colors: light brown, brown, green, and light pink
- Shown in A Really Good Chenille Yarn by ZaddyCrafts in the colorways Gentle (light brown), Cuddly (brown), Witty (green), and Sweet (light pink)

Hook

- 5 mm crochet hook
- Find a full list of notions on page 16, and details for yarn substitutions and hook sizes on page 17.

Special Techniques

- Invisible Fasten Off (page 50)
- Picot Stitch (PS) (page 43)

Kelsea the Cactus Pattern

Starting with light brown:

Round 1. MC, 8sc. (8)

Round 2. 8inc. (16)

Round 3. Work in BLO: sc around. (16)

Rounds 4-5. sc around. (2 rounds of 16)

Round 6. (3sc, inc) x 4. (20)

Rounds 7-8. sc around. (2 rounds of 20)

Add safety eyes between Rounds 6 and 7 with approximately 3 stitches between the eyes.

Round 9. Work in FLO: slst around. (20)

Fasten off with an Invisible Fasten Off into the first st from Round 9 and weave in any yarn tails.

Attach brown yarn to the unused back loops from Round 9.

Round 10. 10dec. (10)

Start stuffing Kelsea the Cactus and continue stuffing as you go.

Round 11. CC to green: (sc, inc) x 5. (15)

Rounds 12-14. sc around. (3 rounds of 15)

Round 15. (sc, dec) x 5. (10)

Round 16. 5dec. (5)

Round 17. CC to light pink: 5PS. (5)

Fasten off, close up the base stitches from the picot stitches, and weave in any yarn tails.

Sharp work! Kelsea the Cactus is complete! Scott the Scorpion is up in a pinch!

Scott the Scorpion

Scott the Scorpion may be small, but they have a flair for the dramatic. They stomp their little legs, wave their pincers in outrage, and flick their tail as though every inconvenience is the worst thing that's ever happened to them. If the sun is too hot, or if the sand shifts the wrong way, Scott will have a monologue ready. Of course, the others secretly find their theatrics very entertaining.

A simple but striking design using a variety of special techniques, this Itty Bitty scorpion is uniquely shaped but easy to make.

Yarn

- Super bulky weight chenille yarn in the color: dark gray

- Shown in A Really Good Chenille Yarn by ZaddyCrafts in the colorway Brave (dark gray)

Hook

- 5 mm crochet hook

- Find a full list of notions on page 16, and details for yarn substitutions and hook sizes on page 17.

Special Techniques

- 2dc Bobble Stitch (B2O) (page 38)

- Multiple Stitches in One Stitch (_in1) (page 47)

- Picot Stitch (PS) (page 43)

Scott the Scorpion Pattern

Starting with dark gray:

Round 1. ch4. (4)

Round 2. Work down the ch starting in the second loop from the hook: 2sc, 3scin1, turn your work and continue working into the other side of your initial ch: 2sc, 3scin1. (10)

Round 3. B2O, sc, B2O, 2inc, 3sc, inc, sc, ch5, work down the ch starting in the third loop from your hook: slst, ch2, work down the ch starting in the third loop from your hook (the same loop as before): slst, 2slst, sc into the same st. (14)

Round 4. 4sc, ch5, work down the ch starting in the third loop from your hook: slst, ch2, work down the ch starting in the third loop from your hook (the same loop as before): slst, 2slst, sc into the next available st of the body, 9sc. (14)

Round 5. sc around (14)

Rounds 6-8. B2O, 2sc, B2O, 10sc. (3 rounds of 14)

Attach safety eyes between Rounds 2 and 3 with approximately 2 stitches between them. These should be above, and lined up with, the two 2dc bobble stitches made on Round 3 respectively.

Start stuffing Scott the Scorpion and continue stuffing as you go, apart from Rounds 10–17 as these form the bend of the tail and any stuffing in here can make it difficult to bend.

Round 9. sc around. (14)

Round 10. dec around. (7)

Round 11. sc around. (7)

Round 12. sc, dec, 4sc. (6)

Rounds 13-17. sc around. (5 rounds of 6)

Round 18. Work in FLO: (sc, inc, sc) x 2. (8)

Round 19. sc around. (8)

Round 20. (sc, dec, sc) x 2. (6)

Round 21. (sc, dec) x 2. (4)

Fasten off and close up the remaining stitches.

Bend your scorpion tail so that the tip lines up over Scott's back. Using some dark gray yarn, fasten the tail to the back of Scott's body with a double knot.

Pinch-perfect! Scott the Scorpion is finished. Let's scurry over to see Jake the Snake before they slither away.

Smooth and graceful, Jake the Snake slithers through the dunes like the desert itself is carrying them. Though small, this Itty Bitty snake loves slipping in and out of sight, appearing suddenly just to make their friends jump before laughing softly at their own trick.

Very beginner-friendly with a fun twist in construction, this mini snake is quick to make and a clever little project for your desert set.

Yarn

- Super bulky weight chenille yarn in the color: yellow
- DK weight cotton yarn in black
- Shown in A Really Good Chenille Yarn by ZaddyCrafts in the colorway Playful (yellow) and Friends Cotton 8/8 by Hobbii in Black

Hook

- 5 mm crochet hook
- Find a full list of notions on page 16, and details for yarn substitutions and hook sizes on page 17.

Jake the Snake Pattern

Body

Starting with yellow:

Round 1. MC, 6sc. (6)

Round 2. (sc, inc) x 3. (9)

Round 3. (sc, inc, sc) x 3. (12)

Rounds 4–6. sc around. (3 rounds of 12)

Add the safety eyes between Rounds 4 and 5, with approximately 4 stitches between the eyes.

Round 7. 6dec. (6)

Round 8. sc around. (6)

Stuff the head portion of the Jake the Snake, and do not stuff any further.

Rounds 9–34. 3sc, work in FLO: 3slst. (26 rounds of 6)

Round 35. (sc, dec) x 2. (4)

Fasten off the yarn and close up the remaining stitches.

Stripes and Curling Effect

With black cotton yarn, starting from the head, we are going to embroider small stripes all the way down the body of Jake the Snake. Each stripe is about 2 rounds apart and 2 stitches in length. Once you reach the end, do not fasten off. Feed a long piece of cotton all the way up the body to where you first entered with the yarn. Pull this yarn tighter, and the body of Jake the Snake should start curling up. Fasten the yarn off by weaving it into the head a few times and tying it to the other end of the yarn. Weave any yarn tails into the body.

Scan for a video tutorial!

Hiss-tory in the making! Jake the Snake is done! Let's slither on over to see how Cameron the Baby Camel is doing.

Cameron the Baby Camel

Yarn

- Super bulky weight chenille yarn in two colors: light brown and brown
- DK weight cotton yarn in black
- Shown in A Really Good Chenille Yarn by ZaddyCrafts in the colorways Gentle (light brown) and Cuddly (brown), and Friends Cotton 8/8 by Hobbii in Black

Hook

- 5 mm crochet hook
- Find a full list of notions on page 16, and details for yarn substitutions and hook sizes on page 17.

Special Techniques

- 3dc Bobble Stitch (B3O) (page 39)
- 4dc Bobble Stitch (B4O) (page 40)
- Color Changing Bobble Stitch (CCB4O/CCB3O) (page 41)
- Picot Stitch (PS) (page 43)
- Seamless Join (SJoin) (page 44)

Cameron the Baby Camel Pattern

Hump

Starting with light brown:

Round 1. MC, 6sc. (6)

Round 2. 6inc. (12)

Round 3. sc around. (12)

Fasten off.

Body

Starting with light brown:

Round 1. MC, 6sc. (6)

Round 2. inc, ch3, work down the chain starting in the second ch from your hook, sc, slst, 2sc into the next available st in the body, 2inc, ch3, work down the chain starting in the second ch from your hook, sc, slst, 2sc into the next available st in the body, inc. (12)

Round 3. (3sc, inc) x 3. (15)

Rounds 4–5. sc around. (2 rounds of 15)

Round 6. 6sc, CCB4O: light brown, 8sc. (15)

Note: The bobble stitches represent the legs for this Itty Bitty. Due to tension, you may need to adjust their placement so they align properly.

Round 7. sc around. (15)

Add safety eyes between Rounds 4 and 5, on either side of the B4O of Round 6, with approximately 4 stitches between the eyes.

Round 8. (sc, dec) x 5. (10)

Rounds 9–10. sc around. (2 rounds of 10)

Start stuffing Cameron the Baby Camel and continue stuffing as you go.

Round 11. SJoin to the Hump, 10sc, SJoin to the Body, 8sc. (22)

Round 12. 6sc, PS, 15sc. (22)

Round 13. sc around. (22)

Round 14. (3sc, dec, 4sc, dec) x 2. (18)

Round 15. 4sc, CCB3O: brown, 3sc, CCB3O: brown, 4sc, CCB3O: brown, 3sc, CCB3O: brown. (18)

Round 16. (sc, dec) x 6. (12)

Round 17. 6dec. (6)

Fasten off and close up the remaining stitches.

Nose

Using black cotton yarn, embroider a small "Y" shape on the brown B4O from Round 6.

Bravo, desert traveler! Cameron the Baby Camel is done! Let's finish strong with Lisa the Lizard.

Lisa the Lizard

Lisa the Lizard is a zippy ball of curiosity, scampering around in search of something new. They're the group's adventurer, always the first to clamber up a dune or peek under a stone to see what's hidden there. Every flick of their tail seems to point toward the next discovery, and they can't help but call out excitedly whenever they stumble across something new.

Lisa is a quick, simple design that's fun to make in a variety of colors. This Itty Bitty lizard is also a good chance to practice amending bobble stitch placements to suit your tension.

Yarn

- Super bulky weight chenille yarn in two colors: green and dark green
- Shown in A Really Good Chenille Yarn by ZaddyCrafts in the colorways Witty (green) and Honest (dark green)

Hook

- 5 mm crochet hook
- Find a full list of notions on page 16, and details for yarn substitutions and hook sizes on page 17.

Special Techniques

- 2dc Bobble Stitch (B2O) (page 38)
- 3dc Bobble Stitch (B3O) (page 39)

Lisa the Lizard Pattern

Body

Starting with green:

Round 1. MC, 6sc. (6)

Round 2. (sc, inc) x 3. (9)

Round 3. (sc, inc, sc) x 3. (12)

Round 4. (sc, inc) x 6. (18)

Round 5. 5sc, B2O, 4sc, B2O, 7sc. (18)

Round 6. sc around. (18)

Round 7. (sc, dec) x 6. (12)

Add the safety eyes between Rounds 5 and 6, with approximately 5 stitches between the eyes. The eyes should sit at the base of the two B2O sts from Round 6.

Start stuffing Lisa the Lizard and continue stuffing as you go.

Round 8. (sc, dec, sc) x 3. (9)

Round 9. (sc, inc, sc) x 3. (12)

Round 10. 3sc, B3O, 7sc, B3O. (12)

> **Note:** The bobble stitches represent the legs for this Itty Bitty. Due to tension, you may need to adjust their placement so they align properly.

Rounds 11-12. sc around. (2 rounds of 12)

Round 13. B3O, 2sc, B3O, 8sc. (12)

Round 14. (sc, dec, sc) x 3. (9)

Round 15. sc around. (9)

Round 16. (sc, dec) x 3. (6)

Round 17. 4sc, dec. (5)

Round 18. 3sc, dec. (4)

Round 19. sc around. (4)

Fasten off the yarn and close up the remaining stitches.

Back Stripes

Using dark green yarn, embroider a series of small stripes down Lisa's back following the Making a Line tutorial on page 56.

You scaled it! With Lisa the Lizard done, our crew of Desert Beauties is complete. Let's get back to civilization.

City Adventures

Although it may be pocket-sized, this city still brims with life. Sidewalks tick with tiny footsteps, rooftops gleam under soft paws, and alleys whisper with squeaks and scuffles. It's an Itty Bitty concrete jungle where adventure hides in every nook and cranny.

Kendall the Cat (page 134) prowls rooftops with quiet confidence, while their loyal friend, Maggz the Dog (page 136), trots at street level. In the alleys, Martino the Mouse (page 140) and Drew the Raccoon (page 142) rummage like a mismatched but inseparable family, squeaking and chittering over every crumb and shiny find. Overhead, Paolo the Pigeon (page 138) soars from lamppost to rooftop, independent and sure of their place in the sky. Together, they turn the city's bustle into a world of friendship, mischief, and small adventures in the concrete jungle.

Kendall the Cat

Kendall the Cat prowls the rooftops like the pint-sized ruler of the city—at least until Maggz the Dog (page 136) comes trotting by. Then the act slips. With a flick of their tail and a mischievous grin, Kendall the Cat darts down into the alley, pouncing just close enough to startle Maggz before darting back up again. They love keeping Maggz guessing, turning every street corner into a game of chase. To everyone else it might look like rivalry, but it's really just Kendall the Cat's way of showing affection.

Switch up the colors to create your own Itty Bitty cat, using classic tabby colors, bright, playful tones, and more. Quick to make and fun to repeat, Kendall is cute and customizable, perfect for building a whole back-alley gang.

Yarn

- Super bulky weight chenille yarn in three colors: warm white, orange, and light pink

- Shown in A Really Good Chenille Yarn by ZaddyCrafts in the colorways Simple (warm white), Charisma (orange), and Sweet (light pink)

Hook

- 5 mm crochet hook

- Find a full list of notions on page 16, and details for yarn substitutions and hook sizes on page 17.

Special Techniques

- 3dc Bobble Stitch (B3O) (page 39)
- Color Changing Bobble Stitch (CCB3O) (page 41)

Kendall the Cat Pattern

Body

Starting with warm white:

Round 1. MC, 6sc. (6)

Round 2. (sc, inc) x 3. (9)

Round 3. CC to orange: (sc, inc, sc) x 3. (12)

Round 4. 6inc, 6sc. (18)

Round 5. (5sc, inc) x 3. (21)

Round 6. 4sc, ch3, work down the chain starting in the third ch from your hook, hdc, skip a st in the body and sc into the next available st, 3sc, ch3, work down the chain starting in the third ch from your hook, hdc, skip a st in the body and sc into the next available st, 4sc, CCB3O: warm white, 3sc, CCB3O: warm white, sc. (21)

Note: The bobble stitches represent the legs for this Itty Bitty. Due to tension, you may need to adjust their placement so they align properly.

Round 7. Making sure you sc into the two skipped sts from Round 6: sc around. (21)

Round 8. 4sc, 3dec, 11sc. (18)

Insert safety eyes between Rounds 4 and 5 with approximately 5 visible stitches between them.

Rounds 9–10. sc around. (2 rounds of 18)

Round 11. 13sc, CCB3O: warm white, 2sc, CCB3O: warm white, sc. (18)

Start stuffing Kendall the Cat and continue stuffing as you go.

Round 12. (sc, dec) x 6. (12)

Round 13. 2dec, ch6, work down the ch starting in the second ch from your hook, 5slst, 4dec. (6)

Fasten off and close up the remaining stitches.

Nose and Whiskers

Using light pink yarn, embroider a small "Y"-shaped nose on the snout of Kendall the Cat.

Using warm white yarn, embroider some small whiskers just below Kendall's eyes.

Purr-fect finish! But where is Kendall's friend Maggz the Dog?

Maggz the Dog

Maggz the Dog is pure sunshine, bounding through the bustle of the city as if it were built just for their tiny paws. They greet strangers, chase pigeons, and nose their way into every corner with uncontainable excitement. Kendall may act like royalty on the rooftops, but Maggz happily plays the fool, always ready to turn the cat's teasing into a game of chase.

Much like Kendall, Maggz is simple and customizable. Try switching up the colors to create your own Itty Bitty dog, whether it's a spotted dalmatian, a golden lab, or a playful pastel pooch. Maggz is a quick, repeatable make that's perfect for creative exploration.

Yarn

- Super bulky weight chenille yarn in two colors: light brown and brown
- Shown in A Really Good Chenille Yarn by ZaddyCrafts in the colorways Gentle (light brown) and Cuddly (brown)

Hook

- 5 mm crochet hook
- Find a full list of notions on page 16, and details for yarn substitutions and hook sizes on page 17.

Special Techniques

- 3dc Bobble Stitch (B3O) (page 39)

Maggz the Dog Pattern

Body

Starting with light brown:

Round 1. MC, 6sc. (6)

Round 2. (sc, inc) x 3. (9)

Round 3. 3inc, 6sc. (12)

Round 4. CC to brown: 2inc, CC to light brown: 4inc, 6sc. (18)

Round 5. CC to brown: inc, 2sc, inc, CC to light brown: 4sc, inc, 2sc, inc, 2sc, dec, 2sc. (21)

Round 6. 2sc, CC to brown: 2sc, ch5, work down the ch starting in the third loop from the hook: dc, hdc, sc, sc into the next available st of the body, sc, CC to light brown: 6sc, ch5, work down the ch starting in the third loop from the hook: dc, hdc, sc, sc into the next available st of the body, 3sc, B3O, 3sc, B3O. (21)

Note: The bobble stitches represent the legs for this Itty Bitty. Due to tension, you may need to adjust their placement so they align properly.

Round 7. sc around. (21)

Round 8. 5sc, 3dec, 10sc. (18)

Rounds 9-10. sc around. (2 rounds of 18)

Round 11. 14sc, B3O, 2sc, B3O. (18)

Add the safety eyes between Rounds 4 and 5, with approximately 4 stitches between the eyes.

Start stuffing Maggz the Dog and continue stuffing as you go.

Round 12. (sc, dec) x 6. (12)

Round 13. 2dec, sc, ch4, work down the ch starting in the 2nd loop from the hook: 3sc, sc into the next available st of the body, 3dec. (7)

Fasten off the yarn and close up the remaining stitches.

Nose

Using brown yarn, embroider a small nose on the end of the snout. This should span across 2 stitches and only loop around twice.

Wow, so fetch! Maggz is done. Now take flight with Paolo the Pigeon.

Paolo the Pigeon

Scan for a 360° view

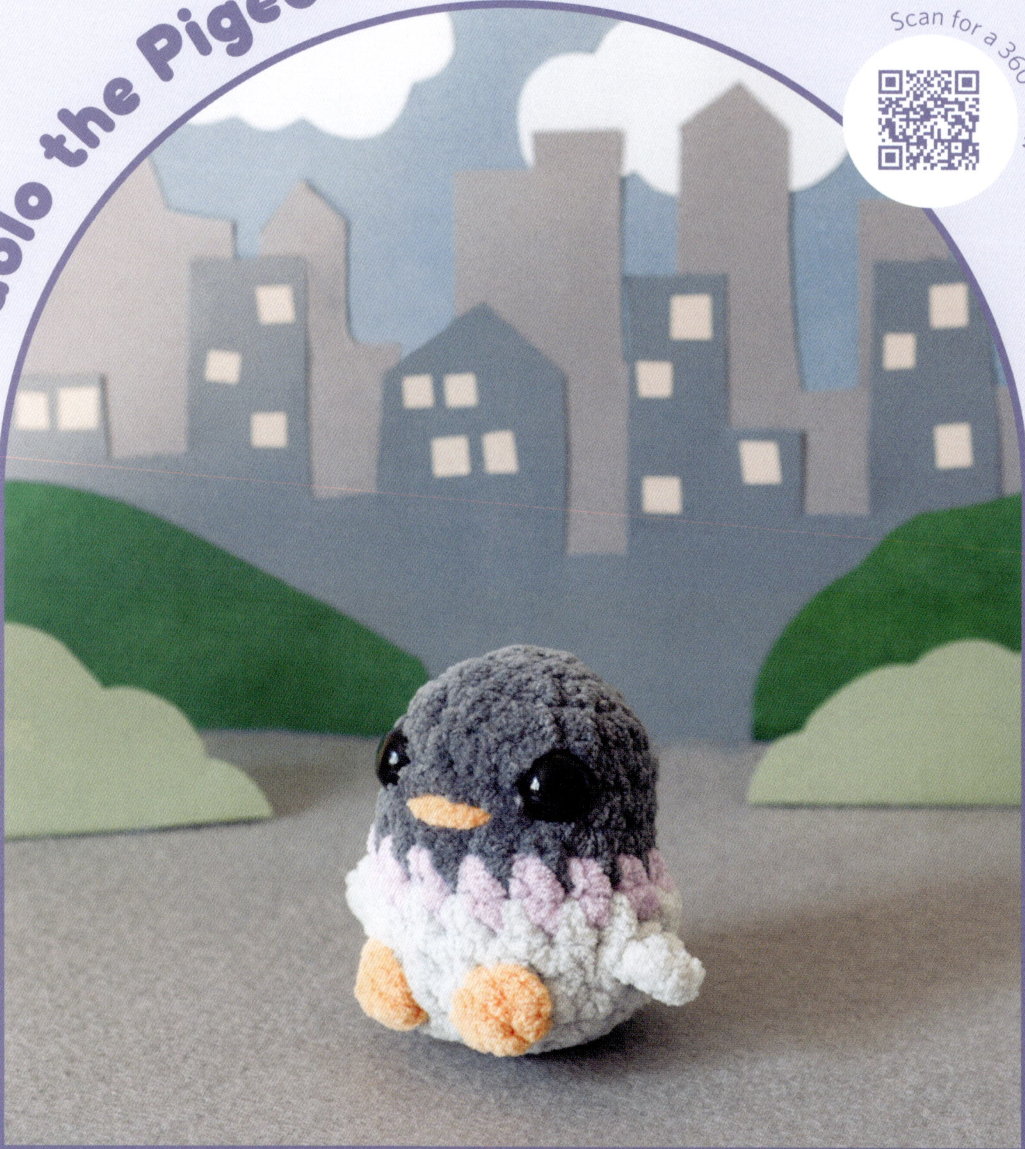

With wings spread wide and chest puffed out, Paolo the Pigeon is the city's smallest broadcaster. They narrate the daily hustle, swooping overhead while describing everything they see below, whether it's Drew and Martino's scavenging, or Kendall and Maggz's latest chase. To the pigeon, it's all worth reporting.

A perfectly sized project, Paolo shares the same approachable qualities as Charlie the Chicken (page 62). Paolo is quick, simple, and delightfully Itty Bitty—a perfect make to start with.

Yarn

- Super bulky weight chenille yarn in four colors: dark gray, light purple, light gray, and orange
- Shown in A Really Good Chenille Yarn by ZaddyCrafts in the colorways Brave (dark gray), Whimsy (light purple), Charming (light gray), and Charisma (orange)

Hook

- 5 mm crochet hook
- Find a full list of notions on page 16, and details for yarn substitutions and hook sizes on page 17.

Special Techniques

- 2dc Bobble Stitch (B2O) (page 38)
- Color Changing Bobble Stitch (CCB2O) (page 41)
- Picot Stitch (PS) (page 43)

Paolo the Pigeon Pattern

Body

Starting with dark gray:

Round 1. MC, 6sc. (6)

Round 2. 6inc. (12)

Round 3. (3sc, inc) x 3. (15)

Rounds 4–6. sc around. (3 rounds of 15)

Round 7. CC to light purple: slst, 14sc. (15)

Round 8. CC to light gray and BLO: inc, work in both loops: 2inc, 2sc, PS, 6sc, PS, 2sc. (18)

Round 9. sc, 4inc, 13sc. (22)

Round 10. 2dec, 2sc, 2dec, 4sc, CCB2O: orange, 2sc, CCB2O: orange, 4sc. (18)

Note: The bobble stitches represent the feet for this Itty Bitty. Due to tension, you may need to adjust their placement so they align properly.

Add the safety eyes between Rounds 4 and 5, with approximately 3 stitches between them.

Start stuffing Paolo the Pigeon and continue stuffing as you go.

Round 11. (sc, dec) x 6. (12)

Round 12. dec x 6. (6)

Fasten off the yarn and close up the remaining stitches.

Beak

With orange, embroider a small beak between the two eyes, between Rounds 5 and 6. This should span across 2 stitches and only loop around twice.

Coo-ol! Paolo the Pigeon is complete! But who took the rest of our breadcrumbs? Was it Martino the Mouse?

Martino the Mouse

Martino the Mouse is small but fearless, zipping through alley cracks and shadows with unmatched speed. Where Drew the Raccoon (page 142) sees adventure, Martino sees opportunity, darting ahead to snag crumbs, shiny wrappers, or whatever catches their sharp little eyes. Martino's brains are the sidekick to Drew's adventurous flair. Drew might make the discoveries look exciting, but Martino makes sure nothing goes to waste.

Quick, cute, and simple in design, Martino is an ideal beginner pattern. They're a tiny, satisfying make that's easy to crochet in one sitting.

Yarn

- Super bulky weight chenille yarn in two colors: light gray and light pink
- Shown in A Really Good Chenille Yarn by ZaddyCrafts in the colorways Charming (light gray) and Sweet (light pink)

Hook

- 5 mm crochet hook
- Find a full list of notions on page 16, and details for yarn substitutions and hook sizes on page 17.

Special Techniques

- 2dc Bobble Stitch (B2O) (page 38)
- Multiple Stitches in One Stitch (_in1) (page 47)
- Surface Crochet (page 51)

Martino the Mouse Pattern

Body

Starting with light gray:

Round 1. MC, 6sc. (6)

Round 2. (sc, inc) x 3. (9)

Round 3. 3inc, 6sc. (12)

Round 4. 6inc, 6sc. (18)

Round 5. 2sc, work in FLO: (hdc, dc)in1, (2dc)in1, (dc, hdc)in1, work in both loops: 3sc, work in FLO: (hdc, dc)in1, (2dc)in1, (dc,hdc)in1, work in both loops: 2sc, B2O, 3sc, B2O. (18)

> **Note**: The bobble stitches represent the legs for this Itty Bitty. Due to tension, you may need to adjust their placement so they align properly.

Round 6. Working into any leftover back loops from Round 5 as you go: sc around. (18)

Rounds 7-8. sc around. (2 rounds of 18)

Round 9. 14sc, B2O, 2sc, B2O. (18)

Insert safety eyes between Rounds 3 and 4 with approximately 5 stitches between them.

Start stuffing Martino the Mouse and keep stuffing as you continue.

Round 10. (sc, dec) x 6. (12)

Round 11. 6dec. (6)

Fasten off and close up the remaining stitches.

Tail

Using surface crochet, attach light pink yarn to the stitches just above the finish of the body.

Row 1. 8ch. (8)

Row 2. Working into the second ch from your hook and continuing to work down the chain, 7slst. (7)

Fasten off and weave in any yarn tails.

Nose

Using light pink yarn, embroider a small nose on Martino's snout.

I'm literally squeaking with joy! Martino the Mouse is done! Let's finish strong with our pal, Drew the Raccoon.

Drew the Raccoon

Drew the Raccoon treats every alley as a new adventure, scurrying into bins and boxes with boundless excitement. What others see as scraps, Drew sees as treasures. Each crust of bread is a feast and each shiny trinket is a rare discovery. Martino the Mouse is always close by, squeaking in delight as they share the spoils of their great finds.

Much like Yohei the Fox (page 80), Drew is full of character with a playful design that's still easy to follow. You'll also get to practice a few simple color changes, making this a small but lively project to round out your city crew.

Yarn

- Super bulky weight chenille yarn in three colors: warm white, light gray, and dark gray

- DK weight cotton yarn in black

- Shown in A Really Good Chenille Yarn by ZaddyCrafts in the colorways Simple (warm white), Charming (light gray), and Brave (dark gray), and Friends Cotton 8/8 by Hobbii in Black

Hook

- 5 mm crochet hook

- Find a full list of notions on page 16, and details for yarn substitutions and hook sizes on page 17.

Special Techniques

- 3dc Bobble Stitch (B3O) (page 39)
- Color Changing Bobble Stitch (CCB3O) (page 41)
- Picot Stitch (PS) (page 43)

Drew the Raccoon Pattern

Body

Starting with warm white:

Round 1. MC, 6sc. (6)

Round 2. (sc, inc) x 3. (9)

Round 3. 3inc, CC to light gray: 6sc. (12)

Round 4. CC to dark gray: 2inc, CC to light gray: 2inc, CC to dark gray: 2inc, CC to light gray: 6sc. (18)

Round 5. CC to dark gray: inc, 2sc, inc, CC to light gray: dec, sc, inc, CC to dark gray: inc, 2sc inc, CC to light gray: dec, 4sc. (21)

Round 6. sc, CC to warm white: 3sc, CC to light gray: sc, PS, 5sc, PS, CC to warm white: 3sc, CC to light gray: sc, CCB3O: dark gray, 3sc, CCB3O: dark gray. (21)

Note: The bobble stitches represent the legs for this Itty Bitty. Due to tension, you may need to adjust their placement so they align properly.

Round 7. sc around. (21)

Round 8. sc5, 3dec, 10sc. (18)

Rounds 9–10. sc around. (2 rounds of 18)

Round 11. 14sc, CCB3O: dark gray, 3sc. (18)

Round 12. CCB3O: dark gray, dec, (sc, dec) x 5. (12)

Add the safety eyes between Rounds 4 and 5, with approximately 4 stitches between the eyes.

Start stuffing Drew the Raccoon and continue stuffing as you go.

Round 13. 6dec. (6)

Round 14. (sc, inc) x 3. (9)

Round 15. CC to dark gray: sc around. (9)

Round 16. CC to light gray: sc around. (9)

Round 17. CC to dark gray: (sc, dec) x 3. (6)

Round 18. sc around. (6)

Fasten off the yarn and close up the remaining stitches.

Nose

Using black cotton yarn, embroider a small nose on the end of Drew's snout. This should span across 2 stitches and only loop around twice. Make sure you do a singular loop from the bottom, pulling it softly to create a small "Y" shape.

So trashy (in a good way)! With Drew joining our pals, our city adventure ends. Let's check in on somewhere a little greener.

Garden Delights

Step into the garden, a place where the ordinary becomes extraordinary. Sunlight glimmers on dew-kissed petals, and the air is alive with gentle chatter, soft buzzing, and the quiet shuffle of tiny feet. It's a small, enchanted world with many stories unfolding beneath its leaves.

Alex the Frog (page 146) hops about with endless energy, always ready to lead the others in a new game. Annemarie the Bee (page 150) hums a steady tune as they tend to the garden. Caylee the Snail (page 152) prefers the slower side of life, gliding contently along, making sure they get all their hellos in before sundown. Nick the Gnome (page 148) insists they're in charge, offering "wise" advice that usually earns a chuckle. And blooming brightly nearby, Jaida the Flower (page 154) sways gently, welcoming everyone into their colorful corner of the garden.

Alex the Frog

Alex the Frog is always on the move, springing from lily pad to stepping stone with boundless energy. They're playful to the core, never missing a chance to splash a friend or turn a simple hop into a daring leap. If there's laughter ringing through the garden, you can bet this little frog is almost always at the center of it, grinning from ear to ear.

A speedy and simple make, perfect for practicing the bobble stitch, this Itty Bitty frog is ideal for a quick crochet fix.

Yarn

- Super bulky weight chenille yarn in two colors: green and mint green

- Shown in A Really Good Chenille Yarn by ZaddyCrafts in the colorways Witty (green) and Clever (mint green)

Hook

- 5 mm crochet hook

- Find a full list of notions on page 16, and details for yarn substitutions and hook sizes on page 17.

Special Techniques

- 3dc Bobble Stitch (B3O) (page 39)

- 4dc Bobble Stitch (B4O) (page 40)

Alex the Frog Pattern

Starting with green:

Round 1. MC, 8sc. (8)

Round 2. 8inc. (16)

Round 3. 3sc, inc, sc, B3O, sc, inc, 2sc, B3O, inc, 3sc, inc. (20)

Round 4. sc around. (20)

Round 5. 6sc, work in FLO: 8sc, work in both loops: 6sc. (20)

Round 6. 6sc, work into the back loops that were unused from Round 5: 8sc, work in both loops: 6sc. (20)

Round 7. 7sc, CC to mint green: 6sc, CC to green: 7sc. (20)

Note: The bobble stitches represent the legs for this Itty Bitty. Due to tension, you may need to adjust their placement so they align properly.

Round 8. 2sc, B3O, 3sc, B3O, CC to mint green: 6sc, CC to green: B3O, 3sc, B3O, 2sc. (20)

Add the safety eyes between Rounds 3 and 4. They are placed just in front of the bobble stitches on Row 3 with approximately 4 stitches between the eyes.

Start stuffing Alex the Frog and continue stuffing as you go.

Round 9. 2sc, CC to mint green: sc, dec, (3sc, dec) x 3. (16)

Round 10. 8dec. (8)

Fasten off and close up the remaining stitches.

Absolutely ribbet-ing work! Alex the Frog is finished. Hop on over to Nick the Gnome next.

Nick the Gnome

Nick the Gnome is never short on grand tales, but every story somehow turns into a punchline. They'll climb onto a flowerpot and announce a daring adventure, only to end with a silly twist that has everyone giggling. Their friends may groan, but they always stick around to hear what nonsense comes next.

A favorite among the Itty Bitty designs, this gnome may be a touch more challenging than some, but it is a fun learning project and absolutely worth the effort.

Yarn

- Super bulky weight chenille yarn in five colors: red, pale peach (or any chosen skin tone), blue, warm white, and black
- Shown in A Really Good Chenille Yarn by ZaddyCrafts in the colorways Vibrant (red), Cheerful (pale peach), Adventurous (blue), Simple (warm white), and Mischief (black)

Hook

- 5 mm crochet hook
- Find a full list of notions on page 16, and details for yarn substitutions and hook sizes on page 17.

Special Techniques

- 2dc Bobble Stitch (B2O) (page 38)
- 3dc Bobble Stitch (B3O) (page 39)
- Color Changing Bobble Stitch (CCB3O) (page 41)
- Invisible Fasten Off (page 50)
- Single Crochet Three Together (sc3tog) (page 49)

Nick the Gnome Pattern

Starting with red:

Round 1. MC, 6sc. (6)

Round 2. (sc, inc) x 3. (9)

Round 3. (sc, inc, sc) x 3. (12)

Round 4. (3sc, inc) x 3. (15)

Round 5. (sc, inc, sc) x 5. (20)

Round 6. Work in FLO: sc around. (20)

Fasten off with an Invisible Fasten Off into the first st of Round 6 and weave in any yarn tails.

Attach pale peach yarn to the first back loop left over from Round 5 and work the next round in those back loops.

Round 7. Work in BLO: sc around. (20)

Round 8. sc around. (20)

Round 9. 10sc, B2O, 9sc. (20)

Round 10. CC to blue and work in BLO: 9slst, CC to warm white and work in both loops: hdcinc, hdc, hdcinc, CC to blue and work in BLO: 8slst. (22)

Round 11. Work in BLO: 7sc, CCB3O: pale peach, inc, CC to warm white and work in both loops: dec, hdc, dec, CC to blue and work in BLO: inc, CCB3O: pale peach, 6sc. (22)

> **Note**: The bobble stitches represent the nose, arms, and legs for this Itty Bitty. Due to tension, you may need to adjust their placement so they align properly.

Round 12. 10sc, work in back loops: sc3tog, work in both loops: 9sc. (20)

Attach safety eyes between Rounds 8 and 9, approximately 4 stitches apart, with the BO from Round 9 in the middle.

Start stuffing Nick the Gnome and continue stuffing as you go.

Round 13. 7sc, CCB3O: black, 3sc, CCB3O: black, 8sc. (20)

Round 14. (3sc, dec) x 4. (16)

Round 15. 8dec. (8)

Fasten off and close up the remaining stitches.

Gnome-body does it quite like a crocheter. Nick the Gnome now has a home. Let's buzz on by Annemarie the Bee.

Annemarie the Bee

Annemarie the Bee zips tirelessly from bloom to bloom, wings buzzing with a cheerful hum. They take their work seriously but wear their busyness with joy, always pausing to check on friends or share a sweet drop of nectar. This little bee is the garden's tireless helper.

A simple and charming design that's perfect for beginners, Annemarie makes a wonderful addition to any Itty Bitty garden crew.

Yarn

- Super bulky weight chenille yarn in three colors: yellow, black, and warm white
- Shown in A Really Good Chenille Yarn by ZaddyCrafts in the colorways Playful (yellow), Mischief (black), and Simple (warm white)

Hook

- 5 mm crochet hook
- Find a full list of notions on page 16, and details for yarn substitutions and hook sizes on page 17.

Special Techniques

- Surface Crochet (page 51)

Annemarie the Bee Pattern

Body

Starting with yellow:

Round 1. MC, 6sc. (6)

Round 2. 6inc. (12)

Round 3. (sc, inc, sc) x 6. (18)

Round 4. sc around. (18)

Round 5. 7sc, CC to black: ch3, work down the ch starting in the second ch from hook, 2slst, CC to yellow: sc into next available st, sc, CC to black: ch3, work down the ch, 2slst, CC to yellow: sc into next available st, 8sc. (18)

Rounds 6–7. sc around. (2 rounds of 18)

Add safety eyes between Rounds 3 and 4, with the small black antennae sticking up between them. There should be approximately 5 stitches between the eyes.

Round 8. 9dec. (9)

Round 9. CC to black and work in FLO: (sc, inc) x 6. (12)

Round 10. sc around. (12)

Round 11. CC to yellow: sc around. (12)

Start stuffing Annemarie the Bee and continue stuffing as you go.

Round 12. sc around. (12)

Round 13. CC to black: sc around. (12)

Round 14. 6dec. (6)

Round 15. (sc, dec) x 2. (4)

Fasten off and close up the remaining stitches.

Wings

Using surface crochet, attach warm white yarn to the center back of the body. Ch4, work down the ch starting in the third ch from the hook, dc, sc, slst into the same st where you first attached the yarn.

Repeat in the exact same spot for a second wing.

Sweet as honey! Annemarie the Bee is done! Let's shell-ebrate with Caylee the Snail.

Caylee the Snail

Caylee the Snail moves at their own pace, leaving a glistening trail that sparkles in the sunlight. They're thoughtful, calm, and one of the first to say hello to others in the garden. Friends often wander over when they need calm company or a kind word from this tiny garden guide.

This design features a more unusual construction, but don't be intimidated. Caylee is still quick, cute, and rewarding, and you'll be wanting to make more and more of them.

Yarn

- Super bulky weight chenille yarn in two colors: light brown and light purple

- Shown in A Really Good Chenille Yarn by ZaddyCrafts in the colorways Gentle (light brown) and Whimsy (light purple)

Hook

- 5 mm crochet hook

- Find a full list of notions on page 16, and details for yarn substitutions and hook sizes on page 17.

Special Techniques

- Surface Crochet (page 51)

Caylee the Snail Pattern

Body

Starting with light brown:

Round 1. MC, 6sc. (6)

Round 2. 2inc, ch3, work down the chain starting in the second loop from the hook: 2slst, sc into the next available st of the body, sc into same st, inc, ch3, work down the chain starting in the second loop from the hook: 2slst, sc into the next available st of the body, sc into same st, inc. (12)

Round 3. (sc, inc) x 3, (inc, sc) x 3. (18)

Rounds 4–7. sc around. (4 rounds of 18)

Round 8. 9dec. (9)

Add safety eyes between Rounds 5 and 6 about 3 stitches apart and stuff the head. You do not need to continue stuffing any further down the body as you go.

Rounds 9–18. sc around. (10 rounds of 9)

Round 19. (sc, dec) x 3. (6)

Fasten off and close up the remaining stitches.

Shell

Starting with light purple:

Round 1. MC, 6sc. (6)

Round 2. 6inc. (12)

Round 3. sc around. (12)

In the next round you are going to join the shell to the body by using surface crochet. You will be crocheting across 2 stitches at a time. The snail's body will be held in front of the shell (the body will be closer to you). Each st will go through one st from back of the body and one st from Round 3 of the shell. To get the curved effect of the body wrapping around the shell, you will be skipping a round of the body with each joining st.

Round 4. Start your joining sts on Round 18 of the body: 4slst, continue your joining sts onto the head portion of the body: 2slst, continue working only into the sts of the shell for the remainder of the shell: 6slst. (12)

Round 5. sc around. (12)

Start stuffing the shell and continue stuffing as you go.

Round 6. 6dec. (6)

Fasten off and close up the remaining stitches.

Shell-ebrations all around! Caylee the Snail is finished. Now let's bloom with Jaida the Flower.

Jaida the Flower

Jaida the Flower always faces the sun, no matter the weather. Even on cloudy days, they find something to smile about. Their cheerful outlook brightens the mood of the whole crew, reminding them that even the smallest bloom can bring joy and patience and help everything grow.

Jaida the Flower features a fun petal-making technique. Jaida is quick to stitch, and even better, you can remake them in endless colors.

Yarn

- Super bulky weight chenille yarn in three colors: yellow, warm white, and mint green

- Shown in A Really Good Chenille Yarn by ZaddyCrafts in the colorways Playful (yellow), Simple (warm white), and Clever (mint green)

Hook

- 5 mm crochet hook

- Find a full list of notions on page 16, and details for yarn substitutions and hook sizes on page 17.

Special Techniques

- Invisible Fasten Off (page 50)

Jaida the Flower Pattern

Starting with yellow:

Round 1. MC, 6sc. (6)

Round 2. 6inc. (12)

Round 3. (sc, inc) x 6. (18)

Round 4. sc around. (18)

Round 5. CC to warm white and work in FLO: slst, (ch3, skip a stitch, slst into next available FL) x 9. Continue directly into Round 6.

Round 6. You will now continue for another round of (ch3, slst into next available FL). Each of these slst will be completed in the leftover front loops from Round 5. As you are crocheting, make sure you are interchanging completing each slst in front and behind the ch3s from the previous round. Fasten off with an Invisible Fasten Off into the first slst of Round 5 and weave in any yarn tails.

Attach mint green yarn to the first leftover back loop from Round 5.

Round 7. Work in the unused back loops from Round 5: sc around. (18)

Attach safety eyes to the yellow side of the flower between Rounds 2 and 3.

Start stuffing Jaida the Flower and continue stuffing as you go.

Round 8. 9dec. (9)

Fasten off and close up the remaining stitches.

May a thousand blossoms bloom! Jaida is all done and wraps up our garden collection. Petal-perfect, don't you think?

Space Explorers

Welcome to the Itty Bitty cosmos, where galaxies sparkle like pinpricks of glitter and comets zip past like playful sparks. Out here, the universe doesn't feel endless. It feels like a pocket-sized playground stitched with light, laughter, and a dash of mischief.

High above the world, the galaxy buzzes with light and motion. Doreen the Sun (page 162) glows warmly at the center, while Minna the Moon (page 164) drifts quietly at her side, calm and steady. Wilfred the Star (page 160) twinkles with flair and Raymond the Rocket (page 166) zooms in daring loops around the group, streaking fire through the sky with a laugh. Chasing after it all is Asher the Alien (page 158), wide-eyed and curious, waving at comets and poking at asteroids as if the whole galaxy were a playground. Together, this little crew turns the endless night into a sparkling stage of adventure and friendship.

Asher the Alien

Asher the Alien zips around the cosmos like the tiniest adventurer in the galaxy. They peek behind asteroids, wave cheerfully at passing comets, and treat every star as a new friend. Their quirky energy keeps the crew laughing, while their sense of wonder makes even the vastest space feel like an Itty Bitty playground.

A favorite among these designs, Asher is great for practicing color changing bobble stitches, but also uses simple techniques that keep the project approachable.

Yarn

- Super bulky weight chenille yarn in three colors: mint green, light gray, and yellow
- Shown in A Really Good Chenille Yarn by ZaddyCrafts in the colorways Clever (mint green), Charming (light gray), and Playful (yellow)

Hook

- 5 mm crochet hook
- Find a full list of notions on page 16, and details for yarn substitutions and hook sizes on page 17.

Special Techniques

- 2dc Bobble Stitch (B2O) (page 38)
- Color Changing Bobble Stitch (CCB2O) (page 41)
- Invisible Fasten Off (page 50)

Asher the Alien Pattern

Starting with mint green:

Round 1. MC, 6sc. (6)

Round 2. 6inc. (12)

Round 3. inc, 2sc, inc, ch4, work down the chain starting in the third chain from the hook, hdc, sc, then sc into the next available stitch in the body, 3sc, ch4, work down the chain starting in the third chain from the hook, hdc, sc, then inc into the next available stitch in the round, 2sc, inc. (16)

Rounds 4–7. sc around. (4 rounds of 16)

Round 8. CC to light gray and work in FLO: (sc, inc) x 8. (24)

Round 9. (sc, CCB2O: yellow, sc, inc) x 6. (30)

Add safety eyes between Rounds 5 and 6, just below the small antennae, with approximately 4 stitches between the eyes.

Start stuffing Asher the Alien and continue stuffing as you go.

Round 10. Work in FLO: sc around. (30)

Fasten off with an Invisible Fasten Off, and weave in any yarn tails.

Attach gray yarn to the unused back loops from Round 10.

Round 11. Work in BLO: (3sc, dec) x 6. (24)

Round 12. (sc, dec) x 8. (16)

Round 13. 8dec. (8)

Fasten off the yarn and close up the remaining stitches.

Stellar job! Asher the Alien is complete. Beam over to Wilfred the Star next.

Wilfred the Star

Wilfred the Star shines with all the confidence of a little light in a big sky. They twinkle proudly when Raymond zooms past or when Asher makes a new discovery, sending out tiny bursts of sparkle to cheer their friends on. Though small, Wilfred's glow adds warmth to the crew, guiding them through the endless night.

This design uses a unique construction method that may be more of a challenge for beginners, but the result is stunning—a rewarding Itty Bitty project that truly shines.

Wilfred the Star Pattern

Points (Make 4)

Starting with yellow:

Round 1a. MC, 6sc. (6)

Round 2a. (sc, inc, sc) x 2. (8)

Round 3a. sc around. (8)

Fasten off.

Body

Rounds 1b–2b. You will now make the fifth point by completing the following: Repeat Rounds 1a–2a of the points.

Round 3b. 7sc, you will now reserve the final st from this round to be used as part of the SJoin for Round 4.

For this next round you will be joining all the points together using the SJoin technique. Once you have connected all five points, the final SJoin will connect the fifth point back to the first point. You will only be working in half of the stitches for each point and then returning to work into the unused stitches later.

Round 4. SJoin using the last st from Round 3, move the stitch marker to be on the second st created from this SJoin, (2sc, SJoin) x 4, 3sc. (20)

Round 5. (3sc, dec) x 4. (16)

Round 6. 8dec. (8)

Fasten off and close up the remaining stitches.

You will now have 20 unused stitches remaining from Round 4. Reattach your yarn to the third stitch of one of the points.

Round 7. (2sc, SJoin) x 5. (20)

Attach safety eyes onto the other side of the star with approximately 2 to 3 stitches between the eyes. Start stuffing Wilfred the Star and continue stuffing as you go.

Round 8. (3sc, dec) x 4. (16)

Round 9. 8dec. (8)

Fasten off and close up the remaining stitches.

Brilliant work! Wilfred the Star looks amazing, but they need a friend to shine bright with. How about Doreen the Sun?

Doreen the Sun

Doreen the Sun is the heart of the group, glowing with warmth and joy. They love to keep everyone close, wrapping their friends in light and laughter. Doreen may be the "biggest" in name, but in this miniature universe they feel like a pocket-sized hug: steady, comforting, and kind. Wherever Doreen floats, the galaxy feels a little cozier.

A simpler design with striking results, Doreen is perfect for practicing essential stitches beyond the single crochet. They're a radiant and accessible Itty Bitty pattern.

Yarn

- Super bulky weight chenille yarn in two colors: yellow and orange
- Shown in A Really Good Chenille Yarn by ZaddyCrafts in the colorways Playful (yellow) and Charisma (orange)

Hook

- 5 mm crochet hook
- Find a full list of notions on page 16, and details for yarn substitutions and hook sizes on page 17.

Special Techniques

- Invisible Fasten Off (page 50)
- Multiple Stitches in One Stitch (_in1) (page 47)

Doreen the Sun Pattern

Starting with yellow:

Round 1. MC, 8sc. (8)

Round 2. 8inc. (16)

Round 3. (sc, inc) x 8. (24)

Round 4. CC to orange and work in FLO: (sc, (hdc, dc, hdc)in1, sc) x 8.

Fasten off with an Invisible Fasten Off into the first st of Round 8 and weave in any yarn tails.

Attach orange yarn to the first unused back loop from Round 4.

Round 5. Work in the unused back loops from Round 4: (sc, dec) x 8. (16)

Attach safety eyes to the yellow side of the Sun between Rounds 2 and 3.

Start stuffing Doreen the Sun and continue stuffing as you go.

Round 6. 8dec. (8)

Fasten off and close up the remaining stitches.

You are on fire! Doreen the Sun is done! Time to orbit on over to Minna the Moon next.

Minna the Moon

Minna the Moon is soft-spoken and dreamy, always drifting alongside their friends with quiet calm. They reflect the brightness of others with gentle grace, often encouraging Wilfred's sparkle or soothing Asher's restless curiosity. Though they seem shy, Minna is always watching, always steady, and always there to support others when they need it.

This design uses a unique construction approach that creates a wonderfully effective result. Minna is a must-have member of your Itty Bitty space crew.

Minna the Moon Pattern

Starting with light gray:

Round 1. MC, 6sc. (6)

Round 2. 6inc. (12)

Round 3. (sc, inc) x 6. (18)

Round 4. (sc, inc) x 9. (27)

Round 5. (sc, inc) x 13, sc. (40)

Round 6. (sc, inc) x 20. (60)

Fold the piece so each st is lined up against another st, creating 30 pairs. slst these pairs together. Once you are about halfway, add safety eyes on either side of the moon between Rounds 3 and 4.

Start stuffing Minna the Moon and continue stuffing as you continue completing the slsts.

Fasten off and close up the remaining stitches.

Moonlight magic! Minna is finished. Now let's prepare for countdown with Raymond the Rocket.

Raymond the Rocket

Raymond the Rocket may be small, but they have the biggest sense of adventure. Always itching to blast off toward the next great discovery, they zoom with flair, leaving trails of fire that light up the void. Raymond may love the thrill of zooming through space, but they never forget to look out for their friends. When Asher the Alien (page 158) drifts too far, Raymond is always ready to go and guide their friend back to the right galaxy.

This sleek and simple design introduces a touch of surface crochet, but it's nothing too tricky, making this Itty Bitty rocket both fun and accessible for beginners and beyond.

Yarn

- Super bulky weight chenille yarn in four colors: red, cool white, orange, and light gray
- Shown in A Really Good Chenille Yarn by ZaddyCrafts in the colorways Vibrant (red), Basic (cool white), Charisma (orange), and Charming (light gray)

Hook

- 5 mm crochet hook
- Find a full list of notions on page 16, and details for yarn substitutions and hook sizes on page 17.

Special Techniques

- Invisible Fasten Off (page 50)
- Surface Crochet (page 51)

Raymond the Rocket Pattern

Rocket

Starting with red:

Round 1. MC, 6sc. (6)

Round 2. (sc, inc) x 3. (9)

Round 3. sc around. (9)

Round 4. CC to cool white: slst, inc, sc, (sc, inc, sc) x 2. (12)

Round 5. sc around. (12)

Round 6. (3sc, inc) x 3. (15)

Rounds 7–10. sc around. (4 rounds of 15)

Round 11. (3sc, dec) x 3. (12)

Attach safety eyes between Rounds 7 and 8 with approximately 3 stitches between the eyes.

Start stuffing Raymond the Rocket and continue stuffing as you go.

Round 12. (sc, dec, sc) x 3. (9)

Round 13. CC to orange and work in BLO: sc around. (9)

Fasten off and close up the remaining stitches.

Attach light gray yarn to the first leftover front loop of Round 13.

Round 14. Work into the unused front loops from Round 13: (sc, inc, sc) x 3. (12)

Fasten off with an Invisible Fasten Off into the first st of Round 14 and weave in any yarn tails.

Wings (Make 2)

Using surface crochet, attach red yarn to the side of the body between Rounds 8 and 9. Work down the side of the rocket, ch1, sc, hdc, ch2, fasten off into the next row below the hdc. Weave in any yarn tails.

Lift-off was a success! Raymond the Rocket completes the cosmic crew. Mission accomplished!

Celebrations Galore

Welcome to the Itty Bitty celebration of all celebrations, where every kind of joy squeezes into one tiny room. From winter sparkle to rainbow pride, love-filled hearts to cozy feasts, this pocket-sized party shines with warmth, laughter, and togetherness.

Claus the Santa (page 178) booms with laughter as he sets down a sack of gifts, insisting everybody take one. Bonnie the Heart (page 170) beams warmly in the middle of the room, reminding the crew that love ties every holiday together. Overhead, Reilly the Rainbow (page 172) shimmers proudly, casting color across the party while cheering for more sparkle. At the buffet, Tim the Turkey (page 176) struts proudly, urging everyone to sit, feast, and be grateful for the company. Meanwhile, Britt the Bat (page 174) swoops in dramatically, making a point that no celebration is complete without a little fun! Together, these unlikely friends create a holiday party where love, pride, gratitude, joy, and playfulness all have a seat at the table.

Bonnie the Heart

Bonnie the Heart glows softly, a tiny reminder that love comes in all shapes and sizes. Gentle and affectionate, they radiate warmth with every beat. Whether they're celebrating friendship, cherishing family, or simply enjoying the joy of being together, this Itty Bitty heart keeps the crew connected.

Bonnie is a simple design that's perfect for practicing the SJoin technique (page 44). Come Valentine's Day, you'll be making a whole bouquet of these Itty Bitty hearts for your loved ones.

Yarn

- Super bulky weight chenille yarn in red
- Shown in A Really Good Chenille Yarn by ZaddyCrafts in the colorway Vibrant (red)

Hook

- 5 mm crochet hook
- Find a full list of notions on page 16, and details for yarn substitutions and hook sizes on page 17.

Special Techniques

- Seamless Join (SJoin) (page 44)

Bonnie the Heart Pattern

Bump 1

Starting with red:

Round 1a. MC, 8sc. (8)

Round 2a. (sc, inc) x 4. (12)

Round 3a. sc around. (12)

Fasten off.

Bump 2

Starting with red:

Rounds 1b–2b. Repeat Rounds 1a–2a of Bump 1.

Round 3b. 11sc, you will now reserve the final st from this round to be used as part of the SJoin for Round 4.

Round 4. SJoin (using the last stitch from Round 3b of Bump 2 and moving the stitch marker accordingly), 11sc, SJoin, 12sc. (24)

Round 5. (3sc, dec, 3sc) x 3. (21)

Round 6. (5sc, dec) x 3. (18)

Round 7. (2sc, dec, 2sc) x 3. (15)

Add safety eyes between Rounds 4 and 5.

Start stuffing Bonnie the Heart and continue stuffing as you go.

Round 8. (3sc, dec) x 3. (12)

Round 9. (sc, dec, sc) x 3. (9)

Round 10. (sc, dec) x 3. (6)

Fasten off and close up the remaining stitches.

Lovely finish! Bonnie the Heart is pumped and ready for more. Reilly the Rainbow next!

Reilly the Rainbow dazzles across the sky, shimmering with every color at once. Bold, bright, and unapologetically proud, Reilly is the life of the party. They are always lifting others up and reminding everyone to celebrate exactly who they are.

A unique design that works up quickly but carries a lot of meaning, small and vibrant Reilly celebrates being your truest self.

Yarn

- Super bulky weight chenille yarn in six colors: purple, blue, green, yellow, orange, and red

- Shown in A Really Good Chenille Yarn by ZaddyCrafts in the colorways Curious (purple), Adventurous (blue), Witty (green), Playful (yellow), Charisma (orange), and Vibrant (red)

Hook

- 5 mm crochet hook

- Find a full list of notions on page 16, and details for yarn substitutions and hook sizes on page 17.

Special Techniques

- Invisible Fasten Off (page 50)

- Multiple Stitches in One Stitch (_in1) (page 47)

Reilly the Rainbow Pattern

Starting with purple:

Round 1. ch6. (6)

Round 2. Work down one side of the ch starting in the second loop: 4sc, 3scin1. Now working up the other side of the ch, 4sc, 3scin1. (14)

Fasten off with an Invisible Fasten Off into the first st of Round 2 and weave in any yarn tails.

Round 3. Attach blue yarn and work in the round: (4sc, 3inc) x 2. (20)

Fasten off with an Invisible Fasten Off into the first st of Round 3 and weave in any yarn tails.

Round 4. Attach green yarn and work in the round: 4sc, (inc, sc) x 3, 4sc, (inc, sc) x 3. (26)

Fasten off with an Invisible Fasten Off into the first st of Round 4 and weave in any yarn tails.

Round 5. Attach yellow yarn and work in the round: 4sc, (sc, inc, sc) x 3, 4sc, (sc, inc, sc) x 3. (32)

Fasten off with an Invisible Fasten Off into the first st of Round 5 and weave in any yarn tails.

Round 6. Attach orange yarn and work in the round: 4sc, (3sc, inc) x 3, 4sc, (3sc, inc) x 3. (38)

Fasten off with an Invisible Fasten Off into the first st of Round 6 and weave in any yarn tails.

Fold the rainbow in half. Each st from one half should line up with a corresponding st from the other half, creating 19 pairs. When you are halfway completed with Round 7, add the safety eyes between Rounds 4 and 5, with approximately 4 stitches between the eyes.

Start stuffing Reilly the Rainbow and continue stuffing as you go.

Round 7. Attach red yarn and work through the sts of each pair: 19sc. (19)

Fasten off the yarn and weave in any yarn tails.

So proud! Reilly is shining bright in their true colors—something Britt the Bat won't see often while hiding in the shadows!

Britt the Bat may look spooky in the flicker of candlelight, but this pocket-sized trickster is all fun and games. Hanging upside down to tell silly stories or sneaking snacks into friends' pockets, Britt is the perfect mix of trick AND treat.

A playful design with a clever wing construction, Britt adds just the right touch of spooky to your collection.

Yarn

- Super bulky weight chenille yarn in light blue
- DK weight cotton yarn in black
- Shown in A Really Good Chenille Yarn by ZaddyCrafts in the colorway Spirited (light blue) and Friends Cotton 8/8 by Hobbii in Black

Hook

- 5 mm crochet hook
- Find a full list of notions on page 16, and details for yarn substitutions and hook sizes on page 17.

Special Techniques

- Picot Stitch (PS) (page 43)

Britt the Bat Pattern

Body

Starting with light blue:

Round 1. MC, 6sc. (6)

Round 2. 6inc. (12)

Round 3. sc, inc, PS, inc, sc, inc, PS, inc, (sc, inc) x 2. (18)

Rounds 4-5. sc around. (2 rounds of 18)

Round 6. 2sc, WING 1, 8sc, WING 2, 6sc. (18) See wing instructions on the right.

In the next round, make sure you are working around the wings so they sit facing forward.

Rounds 7-8. sc around. (2 rounds of 18)

Add safety eyes between Rounds 5 and 6, with approximately 4 stitches between the eyes. Start stuffing Britt the Bat and continue stuffing as you go.

Round 9. (sc, dec) x 6. (12)

Round 10. dec x 6. (6)

Fasten off the yarn and close up the remaining stitches.

Wing Instructions

WING 1

Step 1. ch3, turn and work back down the chain starting in the second chain from the hook: sc, slst, slst into the base of the wing (this is the post of the stitch that you had just chained from). Then work up the wing in the next row.

Step 2. Work in FLO: slst, sc, ch2. Turn and work back down the chain starting in the second chain from the hook: 2sc, slst, slst into the base of the wing. Then work up the wing in the next row.

Step 3. Work in FLO: slst, 2sc, ch2. Turn and work back down the chain starting in the second chain from the hook: 3sc, slst. slst into the base of the wing.

Step 4. sc into the next stitch of the body.

WING 2

Step 1. ch5, turn and work back down the wing starting in the second chain from the hook: 4sc, slst into the base of the wing (this is the post of the stitch that you had just chained from). Then work up the wing in the next row.

Step 2. Work in FLO: 3sc. ch1, turn and work back down the wing, 2sc, slst, slst into the base of the wing. Then work up the wing in the next row.

Step 3. Work in FLO: slst, sc. ch1, turn and work back down the wing, sc, slst, slst into the base of the wing.

Step 4. sc into the next stitch of the body.

Nose

Using black cotton yarn, embroider a small nose between the two eyes. This should span across 2 to 3 stitches between Rounds 6-7 and only loop around twice.

Fang-tastic! Britt the Bat is finished! Gobble on to Tim the Turkey next.

Tim the Turkey

Tim the Turkey struts proudly like a miniature parade all on their own. Tiny feathers puffed, voice booming with laughter, they gather everyone close and remind their friends that gratitude makes any celebration richer. Small but mighty, Tim makes sure no one is left out of the feast.

Tim is a great design for practicing surface crochet, with many of the most common stitches included. They're a festive little project that combines approachability with Itty Bitty charm.

Yarn

- Super bulky weight chenille yarn in four colors: brown, orange, red, and yellow
- Shown in A Really Good Chenille Yarn by ZaddyCrafts in the colorways Cuddly (brown), Charisma (orange), Vibrant (red), and Playful (yellow)

Hook

- 5 mm crochet hook
- Find a full list of notions on page 16, and details for yarn substitutions and hook sizes on page 17.

Special Techniques

- 2dc Bobble Stitch (B2O) (page 38)
- Color Changing Bobble Stitch (CCB2O) (page 41)
- Picot Stitch (PS) (page 43)
- Surface Crochet (page 51)

Tim the Turkey Pattern

Body

Starting with brown:

Round 1. MC, 6sc. (6)

Round 2. 6inc. (12)

Round 3. (3sc, inc) x 3. (15)

Rounds 4–7. sc around. (4 rounds of 15)

Round 8. 3inc, 2sc, PS, 6sc, PS, 2sc. (18)

Round 9. sc, 4inc, 13sc. (22)

Round 10. 2dec, 2sc, 2dec, 4sc, CCB2O: orange, 2sc, CCB2O: orange, 4sc. (18)

Note: The bobble stitches represent the feet for this Itty Bitty. Due to tension, you may need to adjust their placement so they align properly.

Add the safety eyes between Rounds 4 and 5, with approximately 3 stitches between the eyes.

Start stuffing the Tim the Turkey and continue stuffing as you go.

Round 11. (sc, dec) x 6. (12)

Round 12. dec x 6. (6)

Fasten off the yarn and close up the remaining stitches.

Using surface crochet, make five tailfeathers in a row of red, yellow, orange, yellow, and red over Round 9 on the backside of Tim the Turkey.

Tailfeathers (Make 5)

Starting with red, orange, or yellow:

Row 1. ch6. (6)

Row 2. Work down the ch starting in the third loop from the hook: hdc, 2sc, slst into the base of the tailfeathers and fasten off. Weave any yarn tails into the body.

Optional: If your tailfeathers are droopy, use the yarn tails to fasten them upright onto the body.

Beak

With orange, embroider a small beak between the two eyes, between Rounds 5 and 6. This should span across 2 stitches and only loop around twice. Using a small piece of red, embroider a small snood over the edge of the beak.

Feast-worthy finish! Tim the Turkey is complete. Only one more Itty Bitty left—Claus the Santa is your grand finale!

Claus the Santa

Claus the Santa bustles in with a twinkle in their eye and a sack of tiny gifts ready to share. Always laughing, always jolly, Claus is the living spirit of Christmas: generous, joyful, and just a little bit cheeky. They may be small, but this Itty Bitty Santa overflows with festivity.

Claus falls into the mid-level range of difficulty, approachable yet engaging. With joyful details and twinkling charm, this Itty Bitty Santa is the perfect way to finish your celebration crew.

Yarn

- Super bulky weight chenille yarn in four colors: warm white, pale peach (or any chosen skin tone), red, and black
- Shown in A Really Good Chenille Yarn by ZaddyCrafts in the colorways Simple (warm white), Cheerful (pale peach), Vibrant (red), and Mischief (black)

Hook

- 5 mm crochet hook
- Find a full list of notions on page 16, and details for yarn substitutions and hook sizes on page 17.

Special Techniques

- 2dc Bobble Stitch (B2O) (page 38)
- 3dc Bobble Stitch (B3O) (page 39)
- Color Changing Bobble Stitch (CCB3O) (page 41)
- Invisible Fasten Off (page 50)
- Multiple Stitches in One Stitch (_in1) (page 47)

Claus the Santa Pattern

Starting with warm white:

Round 1. MC, 4sc. (4)

Round 2. CC to red: (sc, inc) x 2. (6)

Round 3. (sc, inc) x 3. (9)

Round 4. (sc, inc, sc) x 3. (12)

Round 5. (3sc, inc) x 3. (15)

Round 6. (sc, inc, sc) x 5. (20)

Round 7. CC to warm white and work in FLO: sc around. (20)

Fasten off with an Invisible Fasten Off into the first st of Round 7 and weave in any yarn tails.

Attach pale peach yarn to the first back loop left over from Round 5 and work the next round in those back loops.

Round 8. Work in BLO: sc around. (20)

Round 9. sc around. (20)

Round 10. 10sc, B2O, 9sc. (20)

Round 11. CC to red and work in BLO: 9slst, CC to warm white and work in both loops: hdcinc, hdc, hdcinc, CC to red and work in BLO: 8slst. (22)

Round 12. Work in BLO: 7sc, CCB3O: pale peach, inc, CC to warm white and work in both loops: dec, hdc, dec, CC to red and work in BLO: inc, CCB3O: pale peach, 6sc. (22)

Note: The bobble stitches represent the nose, arms, and legs for this Itty Bitty. Due to tension, you may need to adjust their placement so they align properly.

Round 13. 10sc, work in BLO: 3in1dec, work in both loops: 9sc. (20)

Round 14. CC to warm white and work in FLO: slst around. (20)

Fasten off with an Invisible Fasten Off and weave in any yarn tails. Attach safety eyes between Rounds 8 and 9, approximately 4 stitches apart, with the BO from Round 9 in the middle.

Start stuffing Claus the Santa and continue stuffing as you go.

Attach red yarn to the first back loop from Round 13 and work the next round in the unused back loops.

Round 15. 9sc, CCB3O: black, 4sc, CCB3O: black, 6sc. (20)

Round 16. (3sc, dec) x 4. (16)

Round 17. 8dec. (8)

Fasten off and close up the remaining stitches.

Ho-ho-hooray! Claus the Santa is here with bells on—and our *Itty Bitty Amigurumi* adventure is wrapped up with the most festive cheer!

Acknowledgments

Wow! I actually cannot believe that I am here, right now, writing acknowledgments for a book that truly was a product of chasing my dreams. I am so incredibly grateful to everyone who has been supportive of my journey as a crochet artist. From the kind strangers in public saying "oh, that looks so neat!" at my half-finished projects to the most cherished people in my life just telling me to "give it a go" when seeing how much work I've been putting into the craft: You all mean the absolute world to me and I really cannot thank you enough—but I'm going to try!

First and foremost, I want to thank my friends and family. Mum and Dad, thank you so much for always being there to support me through every moment, for raising me to be a dream chaser, and for being confident that if I'm doing something that makes me happy, then I'm doing well. Thank you to my partner, Thanh, my biggest supporter throughout all of this—my advisor, my confidante, and most of all, the person who kept me grounded whenever it felt like there was too much on my plate. Thank you to my friends for giving me the space to thrive as an artist and for always being ready to jump in and help wherever possible—even if it's just to provide company at the local café.

I also want to give a huge thank you to the publishing team at Page Street for trusting me with this project. I feel so honored and I cannot thank you enough for all the support you've provided along the way. Also, an extra special thank you to Emma, who went above and beyond to create small sets for each plushie to be photographed in.

I would also love to acknowledge my Patreon community. Although I've managed to keep this project a secret for several months, I would not have been able to complete it if it wasn't for your support. I would not have been able to afford rent, food, or the simple necessities if it weren't for my amazing community. Sorry for not telling you about this earlier! I hope you like the surprise, hehe!

Finally, I would like to thank my dearest team of professional crochet artists who not only tested each and every single project in this book, but were also a sounding board for my ideas, and an escape zone when I simply needed a break. Your passion for not only the craft, but also for supporting each other in the crochet community is immeasurable and I simply cannot express how much gratitude I have for this team. Actually, you know what—I think everyone who is reading this book might be able to help me! You can go and support my lovely crochet team by finding them and supporting them on social media: Kendall @kp_crochetcreations, Jake @critterstitch_studios, Ali @alimackenziecrafts, Hege @craftedforcomfort, Reilly @pocketfulloposeys, Kelsea @crochetwithkelsea, Kat @nocturnecat.crochet, Beth @elmtreecrochet, Nicole @nicole_crochets_, Caylee @mommacaylee_creations, Britt @nerdygirlcrochets, Aaron @thecrochetcarpenter, and Millie @redmills_crochet.

And one more massive thank you to someone very special . . . YOU, the reader! You may have been a follower of my work since early 2020, or maybe you joined me for a vlog on YouTube in the past couple of years, scrolled a website and saw that my book looked cute enough to buy, or are simply in a bookstore and having a quick peek! I just want to say thank you for taking the time to indulge yourself in my work. I'm eternally grateful for all the support I've had over the years, and I'm so thankful that I get to share this work back into the community. It's a labor of love that's not just my own—thank you!

About the Author

Hello, it's me, Zac! I am a Melbourne-based crochet designer, amigurumi enthusiast, yarn trader, and the creative force behind Crochet me Zaddy—a brand that celebrates the joy and humor within the crafting world. With my knack for bringing personality and playfulness into every stitch, I have built a vibrant community of crafters who connect over their shared love for cute and simple designs with big personalities.

The heart of my work is a commitment to community. Whether through keeping designs easy, portraying relatable crafting moments online, or creating welcoming spaces for makers, I always try to infuse my sense of humor and creativity into everything I do. My designs are not just about creating cute objects; they're about sparking joy and fostering connections among crafters.

This book, *Itty Bitty Amigurumi,* is a celebration of my love for crafting and a testament to the supportive community that fuels my creativity—so much so that the majority of patterns are named after loved ones and fellow crafters who have supported my journey as a professional crochet artist.

Index